Date Due

The New Schoolhouse

The New Schoolhouse

Literacy, Managers, and Belief

Mary-Ellen Boyle

Westport, Connecticut
London

Library of Congress Cataloging-in-Publication Data

Boyle, Mary-Ellen, 1956–
    The new schoolhouse : literacy, managers, and belief / Mary-Ellen Boyle.
      p. cm.
    Includes bibliographical references and index.
    ISBN 0–275–96879–0 (alk. paper)
    1. Workplace literacy—United States. 2. Employer-supported education—United
States. I. Title.

    LC149.7.B69   2001
    371.2′25—dc21   00–069859

British Library Cataloguing in Publication Data is available.

Library of Congress Catalog Card Number: 00–069859
ISBN: 0–275–96879–0

First published in 2001

Praeger Publishers, 88 Post Road West, Westport, CT 06881
An imprint of Greenwood Publishing Group, Inc.
www.praeger.com

Printed in the United States of America

The paper used in this book complies with the
Permanent Paper Standard issued by the National
Information Standards Organization (Z39.48–1984).

10 9 8 7 6 5 4 3 2 1

To my parents, Mary and John

Contents

Tables

Acknowledgments

First I am grateful to the many managers who took time out of their busy schedules to talk with me about the literacy programs in their organizations. Their candor and commitment were noteworthy, and much appreciated. I also thank the teachers, senior managers, state officials, union leaders, and other professionals in the adult education field with whom I had conversations.

Next, I must acknowledge my own teachers and advisors, who guided me through the initial research and writing: Paul Gray, Sandra Waddock, Eve Spangler, Diane Vaughan, and Brad Googins. Fellow sociologists Elizabeth Sherman and Janet Wirth-Cauchon listened to my earliest ideas, and to them I owe a great deal. As the manuscript progressed, Bill Hoynes and Barbara Bianco provided collegiality, confidence, and caffeine; Maddy Entel a reality check and sense of humor. And, for their guidance on final drafts, not to mention support throughout the writing and publication process, I thank Gary Chaison, Edward Ottensmeyer, and Janet Boguslaw. Finally, while many contributed research and editorial assistance, Elif Satiroglu, Jane Saulnier and Molly Boyle were reliable, detail-oriented, and especially essential.

Most important, my family and friends were a source of joy and support. I am especially appreciative of my son Colin's laughter and understanding, and of my parents' values and examples of perseverance.

Introduction: The New Schoolhouse

"YOU'VE TAUGHT THEM TOO MUCH"

As training coordinator for an insurance company, I was asked to design an educational program for a new type of job. This job would combine data input with risk assessment, and therefore required technical skill as well as knowledge about life insurance. The curriculum included basic information about the industry, as well as specific training in job tasks. My first program graduates (all female and minority) were given permanent positions, and soon showed not only superior capability to get the job done, but also an unusual degree of confidence and ambition. This created a management problem: these workers questioned their superiors, and were frustrated when they weren't promoted quickly. Consequently, I was told, "You've taught them too much." This was suggested in a bemused manner, yet I was surprised. A teacher would have taken, "You've taught them too much" as the highest praise. What was going on here? Why weren't educated, confident employees considered an asset to the organization? Were managers' goals so different than mine as an educator? Could corporate expectations be combined with workers' needs? This experience inspired my return to graduate school, and motivated subsequent reflection about the role of business as educator.

I suggest that this experience of "teaching too much" can be understood as encapsulating several societal debates concerning employer-sponsored adult education, debates that will be analyzed at the level of workplace literacy but that resonate beyond the literacy classroom. These debates concern *purpose* (individual or organizational benefits? skill enhancement or attitude change? liberal learning or technical training?), *allocation* (who attends class? who decides? how much is "too much"? too much knowledge? too much ambition?), and *responsibility* (public or private sector? where are learners' interests represented? what are the consequences of changing the division of responsibility?). Such questions take on renewed urgency as educational credentials become essential to employability and advancement, as traditional boundaries between work and school are blurring, and as the workplace becomes, for many, the primary site for learning basic skills as well as job tasks.

EMPLOYER-SPONSORED EDUCATION

Expenditures on employer-sponsored education and training grew to such an extent during the late 1980s and early 1990s that one observer labeled the workplace "the new schoolhouse."[1] While total spending and overall scope are difficult to assess, the trend is clear: in 1989, estimates showed that employers spent at least as much on education and training as was expended on K-12 public and private education. Statistics from the 1991 National Organizations Study indicate that 43% of those surveyed had increased training expenditures during the prior two-year period—this despite layoffs, restructuring, and other cost-cutting measures. A 1996 survey found that more than two-thirds of the U.S. labor force worked in establishments that offered some kind of formal training; the median training budget was $15,000 (with a mean of nearly $350,000); and the median establishment trained 55.6% of its workforce. And while there is recent evidence that the pace of growth has slowed, total training expenditures continue to increase.[2] Employer-sponsored learning opportunities have become commonplace, taken-for-granted activities in contemporary workplaces.[3]

In this new schoolhouse, most formal learning is job-related (often referred to as training), but a significant portion can be considered education in the broadest sense. These broad learning programs include both enrichment and remedial/compensatory education, and may cover such topics as leadership techniques, statistical process control, or English. Employer sponsorship of basic academics (i.e., reading, writing, and math) is the topic of this book, and these types of educational activities will be referred to as literacy, workplace literacy, and/or basic skills programs. It has been estimated that from 20% to 30% of large U.S. workplaces participate in such efforts.[4] According to the National Alliance of Business, companies in 1998 spent approximately $30 billion on literacy education.[5] And the fastest growing types of programs offer instruction in English to those with limited English proficiency.[6]

Business, government, and labor associations all support the provision of literacy education in the workplace, and money has come from each sector. Government agencies and unions have offered start-up funding for a small percentage of workplace programs, though this involvement has diminished since the mid-1990s. State and federal policy encourages (and in some cases requires) employers to collaborate with community colleges, state education and welfare agencies, labor unions, and other firms.[7] State funders expect that employers will eventually take responsibility for program continuation and for financing. While most employers do take sole responsibility, business groups continue to promote joint efforts, as articulated in the 1999 Conference Board Research Report *Turning Skills into Profit:* "Employers can create partnerships with unions

and local, state, and federal governments as an optimal means to leverage resources to invest in basic skills development" (Bloom and Lafleur 1999:10).

Consequently, employer-sponsored literacy programs unsettle the accepted boundaries of public and private responsibility, and involve the employer
in a new role. In the institutional division of labor, schools, not work organizations, traditionally teach literacy skills. My concern is not just that this is a new
responsibility for employers, but that employer provision of literacy may dis-
place public programs, and, more importantly, that employers may interpret this
role in ways that are not necessarily in the public interest. Given the contention
that employees can be "taught too much," and given greater private sector involvement in education of all types, I wonder about the contours of this new
role, as well as its costs and benefits. As will become apparent in the chapters
that follow, employers have contradictory (and sometimes irrational) justifications for investment in literacy programs, and literacy education has symbolic
value that extends beyond instructional outcomes. More than basic skills are at
stake, as the workplace becomes the new schoolhouse.

My purpose in writing this book is to develop a nuanced understanding
of the consequences of employer-sponsored education, especially as pertains to
literacy. This is not an evaluation study; rather, I will go beyond the issue of
effectiveness to understand the programs' contested meaning for the managers,
the workers, and the society as a whole. At the macro level, I will explore the
blurred boundaries of corporate and state responsibilities made manifest in the
new schoolhouse. These meanings are especially pertinent in the current political and economic environment.

BOUNDARY BLURRING IN THE POLITICAL AND ECONOMIC ENVIRONMENT

The transformation of the economy over the past several decades has
been well documented and exhaustively analyzed. Its causes and consequences
are rhetorically established: globalization, technological innovation, and demographic changes have led to a knowledge-based and service-based economy in
the United States, and subsequently a two-tiered society, with a growing gap
between "haves" and "have nots."[8] Schooling, in the form of educational credentials as well as demonstrable skills, has become an increasingly determinative
factor in this economic order: for the least educated, there is evidence of diminished promotional opportunities, less job security, and ongoing wage stagnation.
Those with college degrees are doing better in all categories.[9] Illiterate adults,
and those with limited English proficiency, are especially vulnerable in the tran-
sition towards a post-industrial, knowledge economy.

Exacerbating these structural economic changes is a neo-liberal political environment in which government power is lessening. As the public sector
diminishes, the private sector increases in power and responsibility. Consequently, market forces are expected to ameliorate economic and social problems
—a shifting of sectoral responsibility commonly referred to as privatization. In
the U.S., privatization is most obvious with regard to traditional state responsi-

bilities in the *social* sector. Depending upon state and local policy, such activities as incarceration, health care, welfare administration, and sanitation may be
administered by for-profit corporations. More commonly, such public functions
may be ceded to private not-for-profit organizations, the growing third sector. In
this economic and political context, the institutional division of labor has become unclear. Boundaries are blurring as corporations manage welfare programs, schools, and prisons. Typically, public funds underwrite these social welfare activities, with private organizations being awarded contracts through competitive bidding. Therefore, despite its name, privatization can still involve both
the market and the state, albeit in an altered configuration of power.

Employer-sponsored literacy education is a unique manifestation of the
privatization trend, yet it reveals the conflicts inherent in blurred configurations
of responsibility. Employer-sponsored literacy programs *seem* straightforward in
that the employer (with occasional state seed money) assumes responsibility for
provision of adult basic education, traditionally a societal function. Yet this is
not privatization as commonly understood, since the employer maintains overriding organizational goals that are not at all related to education—depending
upon the firm, this goal might be manufacturing microchips, providing hospital
care, or distributing shoes. Unlike private prisons or private schools, the new
schoolhouse does not exist to provide a social service at a profit. Rather, educational aims are subordinated to both productivity *and* profit. Given these dual
constraints, it is not clear what type of education the new schoolhouse will provide: will it be the type of broad education needed to sustain the society and
develop the individual, or the narrow type of learning needed by the employer
(who may not want workers who have been "taught too much")? Thus the case
of employer-sponsored literacy education is particularly important as we attempt
to understand the effects of boundary blurring in the contemporary environment.

THE CHANGING CONTEXT OF MANAGERIAL WORK

These new roles and responsibilities of the private sector could not occur without middle managers,[10] yet they are often ignored while attention is
given to the senior executives who wield strategic decision-making power, or to
the workers who must learn new skills. Middle managers give voice to the face-
less "employer," and they are the organization members most knowledgeable
about the new schoolhouse. They are responsible for negotiating the blurred
boundaries: they design, implement, and evaluate literacy education programs.
This book will relate these managers' interpretations, worries, and hopes for the
future, as they become more involved in education.[11]

Managerial work is changing in other ways, too, as firms are buffeted
by the turmoil in the political and economic environment, and face an increasingly competitive global marketplace. Restructuring is the buzzword of greatest
consequence.[12] As work organizations become less hierarchical, openness to
change is expected, and education is implicated. In the lean, flexible organization, responsibility is pushed down, and lower level workers make the types of
decisions that were once the purview of middle managers and supervisors. To do

so, workers ostensibly need new skills and knowledge, as well as new attitudes towards their work and their firms ("soft skills" along with "hard skills"). Thus middle managers must not only manage training endeavors, but also rethink managerial practices as workers become educated and empowered. At the extreme, the middle managers must take into account the fact that their own jobs are threatened, and their position power has become less secure. As will be evident in the pages to follow, involvement in literacy education helps managers cope with these multiple and diffuse pressures. At the same time, managers shape the literacy programs in ways that resonate beyond the walls of the new schoolhouse.

UNDERSTANDING THE NEW SCHOOLHOUSE

Privatization and its consequences, managerial and otherwise, provide the backdrop for several strands of inquiry into the new schoolhouse. First, this study of workplace literacy programs should be considered within the long-standing sociological tradition of debunking.[13] Findings will challenge the expectations of policy makers, corporate executives, adult educators, and academics. By examining seemingly rational behavior, and calling attention to unintended consequences, this book argues that the new schoolhouse works in ways that are contrary to expectations. This critical perspective will augment our knowledge about a variety of subjects: workplace literacy education itself, the institutionalization of culturally valued practices such as education, the symbolic meanings of education to employers and employees, managerial authority in an environment where autonomy and credentials are increasingly valued, and the changing nature of the employment relationship.

Second, the book is informed by a stance that values social justice and is particularly cognizant of the inequities suffered by low-level workers. With economic and social inequalities increasing both in the U.S. and globally, the power and responsibility of corporations must be acknowledged. The poor and less advantaged blame themselves instead of the system, since they have been given freedom and opportunity, and have been shown examples from their ranks that have succeeded. My concerns are both at the macro level and within the firm. As the state retreats from its expected role as protector of the public good, it is not clear that the private sector will sustain or even acknowledge the public good.[14] With regard to employer-sponsored literacy programs, the fear is that social goals will be subverted by employer sponsorship, and that the social problem of illiteracy will not be ameliorated, despite appearances to the contrary. This is an ideological question, but one that can be empirically assessed, which is why this research is necessary. At the same time, I wonder about the ways in which employers might use their new schoolhouse role as a means to control workers and keep them in their place, while appearing to offer opportunity for advancement. There is a rich body of literature on the topic of managerial control, and I will build upon this tradition as I investigate the dance of consent and power made visible by the employer sponsorship of literacy programs.

The constructivist perspective constitutes a third strand of inquiry. From this comes the thesis that the literacy crisis decried by employers and policy makers is in fact more created than real. Thus "manufactured," a crisis benefits certain interest groups at the expense of those whose interests are not as powerful. As Gowen observed, "When major social change occurs, the perception of a literacy crisis is often one of the first indicators" (1992:13). Therefore, the book will raise questions about what the crisis rhetoric presages, asking what social changes *are* threatening, and to whom. This is not to suggest that literacy is an inconsequential or manufactured issue, but rather to explore the possibility that the attention to a certain group's skill deficit may obscure as much as it reveals about social problems and potential solutions.

OVERVIEW OF THE BOOK

Chapter One establishes what I refer to as the education ideology—a set of beliefs about education, deeply rooted in the culture and history of the United States. Education is considered the all-purpose solution to a wide range of social and individual problems, despite evidence that calls such beliefs into question. The need for adult literacy education complicates the faith in education-as-solution, however, and several tensions become evident. Debates about purpose, responsibility, and allocation are outlined in order to build a foundation for critical analysis of the new schoolhouse.

Alongside ideology, context is important, and *Chapter Two* describes adult literacy education in the U.S. The policy, politics, and philosophies of the adult education field are summarized, with particular attention to the ongoing professionalization efforts of adult educators. The history of employer involvement in basic skills education is detailed, as well. A recurrent theme is the tension between employers and educators as boundaries are blurred and the new schoolhouse takes shape.

In *Chapter Three*, attention turns to current workplace literacy programs, and managers' voices are heard. I consider their explanations for supporting literacy education, and place these rationales in an institutional context. I suggest that legitimacy is as important as efficacy in the decision to support literacy education.

Chapter Four looks inside the classroom and examines the programs themselves. I describe the curriculum, the teaching methodologies, time allotted to learning, and student and teacher characteristics. The extent to which learning is narrowly job-related is explored, along with the question of employer control of the learning process.

The next three chapters consider the multiple and contradictory consequences of employer-sponsored literacy education. *Chapter Five* describes managers' perceptions of program outcomes and my assessment of the impact of the literacy experience on individuals and organizations. Attitudinal and symbolic outcomes receive particular attention. *Chapter Six* examines employer-sponsored literacy education in light of what such programs reveal about changes in the employment relationship. This discussion of the new contract crystallizes several earlier concerns of the manuscript: in the new schoolhouse, employers have substituted educational opportunity for job security, accompanied by the caveat that there are "no guarantees." This substitution is more than boundary blurring, and has especially negative consequences for barely literate employees. In *Chapter Seven,* the consequences of workplace literacy are assessed from the perspective of the managers themselves, taking into account the complex and fragmented work environment in which these managers must work in order to implement the education strategy. Middle managers are both agents and subjects of change in the organizations where the education strategy has been selected, and their comments expose this complex and confusing position. Managers of literacy programs provide insight into the larger issues concerning the employer's responsibility for education as well as the professional and organizational conflicts inherent in the provision of such programs.

The book concludes by returning to the concerns raised by the claim that "you've taught them too much." The limits placed upon workplace education programs are contrasted with the high expectations held by employers and policy makers, and the question "who benefits?" is addressed. This is the paradox of the new schoolhouse: unrealistic expectations and inadequate investment. *Chapter Eight* argues that a significant concern with respect to workplace literacy is that such programs create the appearance that social and economic problems are being solved, while at the same time denying attention to the underlying causes and obscuring noneducational solutions. Taking what has been learned into account, policy recommendations are made.

NOTES

1. Michael Useem used this phrase in *Building the Competitive Workforce: Investing in Human Capital for Corporate Success*, edited by Phil Mirvis (New York: John Wiley and Sons, 1993). In a chapter that described company policies on education and training, Useem asserted, "For many young people entering employment, the high school diploma is less symbolic of a completed education than a certificate for transferring to a new schoolhouse, one now managed by the corporation" (118).

2. Establishing training expenditures and prevalence is methodologically challenging. Nonetheless, the numbers substantiating the trend are compiled from the work of numerous researchers, fully cited in the bibliography. See Carnevale and Gainer (1989), Knoke and Kalleberg (1996:171-172), Useem (1993 and 1996:302), Reese (1996), and Cappelli et al. (1997). Additional data is provided by the annual employer surveys completed by the two key practitioner journals: *Journal of the American Society for Training and Development* and *Training Magazine.*

3. At the same time, a counter trend has become evident: the movement to dispense with formal training programs by combining work and learning. This is especially evident at the managerial level, and includes topics that were formerly the purview of organization development and executive education. See Joseph A. Raelin, *Work-Based Learning: The New Frontier of Management Development* (Englewood Cliffs, NJ: Pren-

tice Hall, 2000). Alternatively, some analysts have suggested that the new economy discourages investment in employee training, since so many employees are contingent, and work has intensified for the permanent employees. See Peter Cappelli, Laurie Bassi, Harry Katz, David Knoke, Paul Osterman, and Michael Useem, *Change at Work* (New York: Oxford University Press, 1997).

4. Accurate data concerning workplace literacy programs are even more difficult to determine than overall training statistics. I have cited the 1996 meta-analysis "Illiteracy at Work," by Shelley Reese in *American Demographics* 18: 14-15. I also relied upon the 1995 National Employer Survey, conducted by the National Center on the Educational Quality of the Workforce (*First Findings From The EQW National Employer Survey*. Washington, DC: U.S. Dept. of Education, Office of Educational Research and Improvement, Educational Resources Information Center, 1995). Finally, I tabulated data reported in *Training Magazine's* annual "Industry Reports," 1990-1999.

5. These figures are from "White Paper for 1999 National Literacy Forum," *National Institute for Literacy Policy Update* (April 12, 1999). The NIFL is a useful clearinghouse for information about adult literacy; publishing regular policy updates (print and electronic) and sponsoring an active list serve for practitioners and academics. See <http://novel.nifl.gov>. Also, Chapter Two includes further discussion of federal involvement in literacy.

6. English literacy for "those with limited English proficiency" (the accepted phrasing) is the nation's fastest growing and largest adult education program for the third consecutive year, according to *A.L.L. Points Bulletin*, a newsletter published by the Division of Adult Education and Literacy, Office of Vocational and Adult Education, U.S. Dept. of Education (November 18, 1999). Educational programs for those with limited English proficiency are traditionally referred to as ESL (English as a Second Language), although the acronym ESOL (English for Speakers of Other Languages) is gaining popularity. I will use the more common "ESL" in this book.

7. See, among others, U.S. Congress, Office of Technology Assessment, *Worker Training: Competing in the New Economy* (Washington, DC: U.S. Government Printing Office, 1990); Massachusetts Executive Office of Economic Affairs, *Guidebook for Massachusetts Workplace Education Initiative* (Boston: 1987); and Forrest P. Chisman, *The Missing Link: Workplace Education in Small Business* (Washington, DC: Southport Institute for Policy Analysis, 1992).

8. According to Congressional Budget Office data, the top one-fifth of American households with the highest income now earns half of all the income in the U.S., a share that has risen significantly since 1977. Similar findings have been widely reported over the past several years. For graphs and analyses, see David C. Johnston, "Gap Between Rich and Poor Found Substantially Wider," *New York Times* (September 5, 1999:14).

9. Refer to the National Organizations Study, the basis of Arne L. Kalleberg, et al., eds., *Organizations in America: Analyzing Their Structures and Human Resource Practices* (Thousand Oaks: Sage, 1996). The Bureau of the Census in "The American Community Survey," 1997, confirmed these findings.

10. The managers' titles varied, with most in the human resources/training departments and a few with operational responsibility. For purposes of this book, they will be referred to collectively as "middle managers," though this may be more or less accurate, depending upon the organization. I argue that they have more in common with each other than not, especially as they relate to the literacy program.

11. Two primary methods were used to study the new schoolhouse: manager interviews and participant observation at the state planning level. Working from a directory of Massachusetts's employment organizations that offered literacy education on-site

during 1994 and 1995, I selected 30 firms: 10 manufacturing, 10 service, and 10 health care entities. Firm sizes ranged, with median being 500 employees. While nearly half of these firms began their literacy programs with state or federal grant money, the organizations themselves provided the main financial support in all cases. In each workplace, I interviewed the manager who had the most direct responsibility for literacy programming. During the interviews, managers were asked to describe their educational programs as to motivations, educational processes, and outcomes. They were then presented with a set of open-ended questions regarding the employer's role as educator, the meaning of these programs for the managers themselves and the social problem of illiteracy.

The interviews were supplemented with classroom observation, informal conversations with teachers and state program administrators, and analysis of curricular materials used in the workplace literacy classroom and practitioner literature. I was also employed during the early 1990s as a grant manager for a Massachusetts employment and training agency, where I was responsible for administering various funding streams for workplace literacy programs. During this time I not only reviewed paper work pertaining to the programs, but also attended meetings of educational providers and employers, and visited numerous community and workplace programs to collect evaluation data.

Given the qualitative nature of the methods, a caveat about representativeness is called for. These findings from the manager interviews should be considered illustrative rather than definitive, given both the sample size and survey format. It should be emphasized that the study was designed to understand meaning, not frequency or tendency, though in several instances frequency is reported.

12. These changes are not unidirectional; rather, they vary over time and among different firms. Bennett Harrison and Marcus Weiss, in *Workforce Development Networks* (Thousand Oaks: Sage Publications, 1998) described the variety: "What this amounts to, in practice, is a proliferation of different forms of work organization, blurring the traditional distinctions between 'core' and 'periphery,' 'permanent' and 'contingent,' 'inside' and 'outside,' employees, and 'primary' and 'secondary' labor markets" (18).

13. Alexander Portes describes this spirit, and places it in disciplinary context in his 1999 presidential address. It is reprinted as "The Hidden Abode: Sociology as Analysis of the Unexpected," *American Sociological Review* 65 (February 2000): 1-18.

14. It is important to acknowledge that "The idea of the public good is indeed vexed and contested in that researchers need to ask questions like, 'Which public?' and 'For whose good?' " as is stated in the editors' introduction to *Private Action and Public Good*, edited by Walter W. Powell and Elizabeth S. Clemens (New Haven: Yale University Press, 1998): xiv. I take up these questions in my concluding chapter.

1

Education, Ideology, and Work

We recognize that education is a good thing. It is a right.

Director of Training,
Community Hospital

We see this involvement in education as a partnership for the future.
Americans resent things going offshore. We can hang together or hang
separately.

Personnel Manager,
Tool Manufacturer

To stay competitive, companies have to educate to do the job right.

Manager of Human Resources,
Distribution Firm

Beliefs about education run deep in American culture: the belief that education
is a fundamental right, and a "good thing," as alluded to by the first manager
quoted above; the belief that education will protect against foreign competitors
and prepare us for the future, as the second statement shows; and the belief that
education is essential to success, as indicated by the third manager. Even as
"teaching too much" might be lamented, education is considered one solution to
problems of individual prosperity and economic competitiveness, and education
is blamed when success in these arenas is elusive. I stress that these are beliefs,
not truths, in order to begin the discussion of the new schoolhouse with an
acknowledgment that much what management asserts about the necessity and
functionality of education is not based in the objective calculus of a cost-benefit
analysis—rather, as the selected quotes illustrate, such assertions are subjective,
rooted in the larger culture, and relatively unexamined. These beliefs are powerful and ubiquitous in the United States, where education is highly valued and
strongly institutionalized.

Establishing the value accorded these beliefs is a central goal of this chapter. I will recount debates concerning purpose, access, and responsibility, and make two related arguments: first, that the *power* of the educational ideology results in a set of intended and unintended consequences, especially noteworthy when employers sponsor literacy; and second, the *nature* of cultural beliefs about education contributes to the boundary blurring that must be foregrounded in attempts to understand the social impact of the new schoolhouse. This chapter will call into question the American assumption that education is an all-purpose solution to economic and social problems. In this context, employer involvement in literacy education is presented as a controversial and potentially disquieting development.

EDUCATION AND AMERICAN VALUES

Beliefs concerning education constitute a basic ideology in the United States.[1] This ideology pervades public policy discussions and influences organizational decision-making, so much so that education is considered the solution to social problems ranging from AIDS to poverty to a company's ability to keep jobs from moving out of the country. That education has taken on such a seminal role is rarely problematized. The power of these beliefs can be explained by their resonance with three key tenets of American identity: individualism, equality, and opportunity.

The United States is an individualistic culture.[2] The belief is that individuals succeed or fail based on their own merits and achievements, rather than because of ascribed characteristics (such as gender, race, ethnicity, or family) or structural factors (such as monetary policy, economic cycles, or the organization of the labor market). Americans celebrate Horatio Alger and Bill Gates as tough individualists. The educational and economic systems are structured to give individuals opportunities to achieve success on their own terms. Schools take individual development as the goal, and grades are awarded to individuals. Likewise, at work, individuals are rewarded for their own accomplishments, and are held responsible for their future security, despite the occasional paternalistic employer and limited government safety net. The paradoxes inherent in a society of individuals have long engaged sociologists and students of American culture. Suffice it to say that belief in individualism exists in contradiction with another core belief, equality.

"All men are created equal," states the Bill of Rights, and belief in equality deeply influences institutions and culture in the United States. But the ideal has proven much easier to envision than the reality, even though the American system attempts to assure equality through universal access to education and through legal protections. Economic equality is increasingly elusive in the polarized economy, and while legal advances continue to protect against *unequal* treatment on the basis of gender, race, religion, or other protected characteristics, this goal is far from being attained. Yet belief in equality persists: nearly constant calls for public school reform can be understood as resulting from cultural concern about unequal opportunities for achievement, along with unequal results of schooling, particularly among those least economically advantaged. Moreover, though workplaces are not structures of equality, managers exhibit attitudes of fairness and reveal their beliefs in the ideals of equality, as will become evident in their justification of literacy education.

These beliefs in individualism and equality are operationalized through opportunity—the opportunity to learn and to work. Education scholar Caroline Hodges Persell describes the "creed":

> The United States, perhaps more than any other society, holds as a cherished ideology the concept of a fresh start for each generation. Young people, the creed goes, should be given a fair chance to be all they can be. For a nation of immigrants, two opportunities are essential—the opportunity to learn the language, the culture, and skills, and the opportunity to work. (1991:285)

This essential first opportunity, "to learn," forms the rationale behind state-sponsored education and the requirement of mandatory school attendance for youth. Education has long been considered the great equalizer, and schools are the crucibles where the ideals of individualism and equality are heated and potentially realized.[3] The second opportunity, "to work," has increasingly become reliant upon educational credentials, causing these two opportunities to become intertwined. Here is where the creed falters, and fairness is compromised. Education cannot be limited to "young people" in the current political and economic climate. The fact is that many adults remain illiterate and, without educational credentials, are denied a fair chance at work. Yet, the nature of the education ideology is such that it is difficult to alter the distribution of resources between children and adults. While education may be "a good thing," the belief is that children, not adults, deserve public support and renewed opportunities. One unintended consequence is the lack of opportunity for illiterate adults. Adult basic education confounds taken-for-granted assumptions about the purposes of schooling, and highlights an enduring tension between the two essential activities of learning and working.

THE PURPOSES OF EDUCATION

Education for What?

The debate about the purpose of education in Western civilization can be traced to antiquity, to the differing philosophical perspectives of Sophocles and Socrates. This debate is alive today, as business leaders, educators, and policy makers disagree about the purpose of employer-sponsored education. Should such learning be entirely pragmatic and work-related, or should such learning focus on individual development beyond the worker identity? In ancient times, the Sophists were paid teachers who believed that learning should be pragmatic. They trained youth in rhetoric, politics, and law, with some attention to arts, crafts, and other such applied subjects. Their goal was to teach people to live successfully; they did not ask what living successfully meant. In contrast, those who advocated the Socratic philosophy believed that the purpose of education was to enable the learner to ask, and answer, "value" questions, especially questions concerning the right way of life. To Socrates, the goal was a life of virtue, accomplished through the search for the good. Learning was justified "for its own sake" if it assisted in that search, and, while pragmatic education was not eschewed, it was not the priority.

In the Socratic worldview, since the future cannot be anticipated, all is possible, and therefore universal truths are what must be pursued through formal learning. In the pragmatic worldview, there is the sense that the future can be anticipated, and education should prepare learners for such.[4] The Sophist and Socratic perspectives on the purpose of education obviously extend beyond the question of the nature of schooling or content of curriculum to larger philosophical questions about the purpose of life, and these fundamental questions continue to resonate thousands of years hence. One legacy of this debate is two types of educational purpose—*liberal* (derived from, though not completely mirroring, the Socratic educational philosophy of inquiry) and *pragmatic* (in the Sophist tradition, education that has a specific end in mind). These are ideal types—truest in the abstract; they can also be considered ends of a continuum. As such, they are useful concepts upon which to build an exploration of the consequences of employer sponsorship of education. Liberal education is typically associated with a broad curriculum and "higher" levels of learning, and pragmatic with a narrow curriculum that is directly applicable to practical concerns, such as work. Employers ostensibly need only a few workers who are educated in the liberal tradition.[5] But pragmatic learning *is* valued by employers, who provide such education for their employees under the label of training. Literacy, seemingly a precursor to both liberal and pragmatic learning, becomes controversial when purpose is debated because the basic skills curriculum can be more or less liberal or pragmatic.

The question of "education for what?" has taken on unique characteristics in the United States, now and in the past. Though the liberal and pragmatic ends of the continuum encapsulate core values, pragmatism reigns in policy discussions. Consequently, adult education often has a pragmatic, work-related rationale, despite educators' efforts to broaden the mandate. This is not without precedent—Benjamin Franklin and Thomas Jefferson were two founding fathers most interested in education, and they believed that democracy required educating the masses. Yet their purposes differed: Franklin wanted to train students in pragmatic tasks that led to economic independence, while Jefferson was more concerned with teaching them "how to work out their greatest happiness as citizens"—the liberal approach. This philosophical schism was echoed in the early efforts to justify universal public education, and, though both agreed on its necessity, their disparate purposes resulted in some of the contradictions obvious today. As cultural commentator Nicholas Lehman describes it, "educators of a Jeffersonian bent...learned to play the Franklin card" (1995:14-15)—stressing the practical benefits of education as a way of persuading the public to pay taxes for it. This compromise created a paradoxical situation—a "bait and switch," to offer a marketing metaphor. Educators were forced to use pragmatic arguments, rather than justifications based on higher values, in order to bring about their avowedly nonpragmatic end result of education for the good life and "their greatest happiness." This pragmatic justification continued to be victorious throughout the industrial era, as schools were designed to prepare future factory workers and citizens, with so-called higher values quietly sustained by "school men," not "business men," to use the parlance of the times.

The tension endures today, with the pragmatic "card" often used to obtain funding, while educators of a Jeffersonian bent continue to teach in a liberal manner once they close their classroom doors. The field of compensatory (basic skills) education for adults is particularly problematic, and even something so seemingly basic as literacy engenders controversy: some educators and policy makers resist policies that focus on the workplace, while some labor leaders and employers advocate literacy programs that are at work and about work. Those who believe in learning for learning's sake position themselves against those who advocate for education that is solely pragmatic; to certain decision makers, it is conceivable to "teach too much," while others promote life-long learning.

Notwithstanding the philosophical and policy debates, the trend among adults themselves is to seek out education that will improve their economic prospects. Whether this learning is pragmatic or liberal is less important than whether the learning results in credentials, since the diploma or certificate is seen as the path to a more secure future.[6] Particularly for those who lack a college degree, education is an unquestioned American value, and the type of education is often not as consequential as the fact of its ideological power.

The Paradox of the Education Solution

One answer to the "education for what?" question, is "education for everything." Whether liberal or pragmatic, education in the U.S. is a panacea, and also a scapegoat. Solutions to social problems often include education, and schools are blamed when social problems persist. More and better education becomes government policy, and requirements for such can be seen in public health programs, prison rehabilitation efforts, and scholarships for disadvantaged and minority students. Education-as-solution is linked to core beliefs (and contradictions) of American culture, particularly the cherished creed linking individualism, equality, and opportunity.

Individuals have internalized the education-as-solution belief, explaining the demand for adult education and the nearly constant calls for educational reform. Yet societal commitment to the education solution is rather thin, and limited to pragmatic rather than liberal goals. Paradoxically, despite great expectations, public funding for education is constrained, especially when it comes to adults, and particularly so in the current political climate: funding for prisoner education is embattled, as is money for drug abuse prevention and sex education. The limitation can be indirect, too: recent changes to the welfare system decrease the possibility that recipients will be able to obtain enough education to keep them out of poverty. So although education is seen as a solution, it must result in a quick and inexpensive fix, or else it becomes the scapegoat. Such a contradiction places unrealistic demands on the system, as well as on individuals themselves. Yet the contradiction does not temper the demand—and employers have adopted the education solution to address workplace and competitiveness concerns. Clearly, the belief in education transcends public/private boundaries, as is exemplified by the new schoolhouse.

The belief that education should solve "everything," and do so quickly, is illogical and potentially damaging on several accounts. First, the belief serves to obscure alternative explanations for social problems, and such incomplete explanations discourage creative, substantial, and ultimately more effective solutions. Second, the high expectations placed on the education solution result in unattainable demands on individuals and educators. People become confused and discouraged, and blame themselves rather than the flawed policies or in-adequate funding. Third, in the current political environment, education-as-solution is subject to market forces and private sector standards, contradicting egalitarian ideals and the conviction that education is a public good.[7] Whether these standards are adequate (or, indeed, ideal) is one of the questions addressed by this book. Even so, this is not to suggest that education is a trivial aspect of efforts to ameliorate problems such as AIDS or poverty or underemployment. Rather, to reiterate, the education solution alone is not enough.

Education, Work, and the Economy

Nowhere is the ideology of education-as-solution more evident than where economics are concerned. The relationship between the amount of educa-tion and economic success is "proven" through aggregate survey data at levels of analyses ranging from the individual to the nation state, and is consistent across cultures and over time, according to labor economists. Years of schooling and additional degrees correlate with increased lifetime earnings; companies that expend more on education and training earn greater profits; and nations that have high education levels have stronger GNPs.[8] Consequently, when the prob-lem is economic competitiveness (on any level), managers, policymakers, and workers look to education as the cause and the solution. The contours of this solution are well known: vocational and occupational education programs for youth are strengthened, governments increase "second chance" educational ex-penditures for displaced and incumbent workers, and corporations go so far as to create their own universities for existing employees.[9, 10]

Yet the link between education and the economy is not straightforward, despite beliefs to the contrary. When data are disaggregated, the causative rela-tionship is less certain. Correlation does not equal causation, and labor econo-mists have not established exactly *how* education is translated to enhanced pro-ductivity, despite decades of attempts.[11] For individuals, credentials and knowl-edge both appear to result in better pay, though again the mechanisms are unclear. The puzzle is complicated by the fact that too much education can also be a problem, causing dissatisfaction and lowered productivity among those whose abilities surpass those needed by their jobs. Such "overeducation" of the workforce has been documented consistently for nearly thirty years.[12] Estimates of incidence vary depending upon the definition of the variables, but the general consensus among the labor economists working in this field is that overeducation affects approximately 40% of the working population (not taking into account the overeducated unemployed). As a consequence, it has been suggested that education is as much symbolic as real in its effects on economic prosperity.

Regardless, the idea that there is a direct connection between education and economic success resonates with deeply felt American beliefs about individual possibility and equal opportunity. Accordingly, education as the solution to economic problems has been reified, with negative consequences for those without diploma-certified skills and knowledge. It is especially difficult to question the truth of this assumption, since alternative explanations for success and failure are at odds with the education ideology. U.S. education and employment policies are rooted in these "truths," and as these policies increasingly become the responsibility of the private rather than public sector, it is important to consider the power of the ideology, as well as the implications of the fallacious assumptions about causation.

The power of the education ideology as it relates to economic competitiveness is most apparent in two supposed problems: the skill gap and the failure of the public schools. Both of these have been subject to scholarly debunking, yet the ideology holds sway. First, to remain successful in the information- and knowledge-based economy, companies are exhorted to be flexible, high performing, learning organizations.[13] To do so, they ostensibly need highly skilled workers. New types of work, new ways of organizing work, and a new employment contract also presumably demand new skills, again to be imparted through more and better education.[14] A "skill gap" is believed to exist between existing workers and these new work demands, particularly in industries reliant upon technology and applied knowledge.

The skill gap is not just about narrow technological expertise, though this is a significant aspect. In the knowledge-based economy, brains have frequently replaced brawn as the technique of production, and great attention is being given to the thinking skills needed by those who were once simply manual workers. "Smart workers, [and] smart work" are called for, to quote the title of an influential policy report (Bassi 1992). Furthermore, technological advances have brought about a decontextualizing of work, moving it into an abstract realm and adding the mandate to relearn and unlearn whenever new technology is introduced.[15] Such conceptual skills don't lend themselves to simple training schemes, and might be best instilled by liberal rather than pragmatic types of education.

Additionally, "soft" skills—attitudinal and social—are included in discussions of the skill gap. The concern is that future employees have a "good attitude," can get to work on time, and can adapt to constantly changing and intensifying work demands.[16] And since the work changes often take place in flattened, team-based organizations, nonmanagers are expected to make decisions and carry out complex tasks, increasing the communicative demands on lower level workers.[17] Therefore, employers want soft-skills education, too, in order to bring about desired work attitudes and to enhance the social abilities that lubricate effective communication. If the skill gap is ostensibly the cause of competitiveness problems, then more and better education, of all types, is thought to be the cure.[18]

The underlying belief is that the failure of the public schools has contributed to the competitiveness and skill gap problems. This is not a new idea, yet is uniquely constructed in the contemporary era: building upon the 1983 publication of *A Nation at Risk*, and subsequent government-sponsored studies, a feared decline in national competitiveness has framed the appeal for school reform. During that decade, the U.S. was considered to be at risk of losing its economic dominance in the world because of the educational deficiencies of its workforce, and the schools were held accountable for the productivity failings of the American workers and firms.[19] In the current climate of economic prosperity, the causes and solutions are the same, though the emphasis is now on economic inequities. Not all have benefited equally from the soaring stock market and low unemployment, and again the skill gap/school failure explanation is ubiquitous, and the education-solution called upon. Income disparities correlate with credentials and years of education, if not actual skills, so fairer educational opportunities and school reform are demanded.

The debates about future work skills and the continual efforts to reform schools do nothing to dispel the belief that more education will result in a stronger economy. The nature of the educational ideology is such that alternative approaches to the competitiveness problems are not considered. Again, unrealistically high expectations are placed on educational systems, and on the individuals expected to take advantage of educational opportunities. Whether real or symbolic, these expectations are especially felt by those most disadvantaged in the current economic climate, the illiterate adults. The critical question becomes "who should be responsible for adult education?" Given the lack of clarity about purpose, the answers are especially contradictory.

WHO SHOULD BE RESPONSIBLE?

Since foundational education is considered a public good, the state is believed to be responsible for its provision.[20] Even in this era of privatization and school choice, the public sector is expected to provide the basic skills needed to prepare individuals to be citizens and workers. This presumption of state responsibility is not controversial, and state funding accompanies the state mandate—basic education is free and compulsory, for *children*. And when the education-solution is deemed necessary to solve social problems, the public usually pays. These beliefs are in keeping with the high value placed on education by Americans—and reflect longstanding institutional divisions of labor and responsibility.

Responsibility is not so clear when it comes to adults in need of basic skills, however. The debate about purpose becomes significant. In the U.S. belief system, education is intended for children. Since the presumption is that people will gain the skills they need while they are young, illiterate adults pose philosophical as well as practical problems. Should adults have the same broad opportunities as youth, or should their education be limited to the pragmatic "amount" needed to keep them out of poverty? Moreover, what is the state's responsibility?

Unquestioned belief in the value of education conflicts with beliefs about individual responsibility and the limits of equal opportunity. There are two perspectives: some believe that the state should be responsible, since the society as a whole will benefit from educated, employable citizenry, and age should not matter. Part of the rationale supporting this view revolves around the "right" to basic education and literacy, as alluded to by the manager whose quote opened the chapter, and as supported by numerous adult education advocates. The alternative perspective is that the individuals themselves are now responsible, since they were given the opportunity to be educated (in their youth) and apparently wasted it. This view presumes that all adults had such opportunities, which is not necessarily true for immigrants. Neither of these views suggests that employers should be responsible, though in the neo-liberal policy environment, this is increasingly the case. Employers' involvement in literacy education clearly confounds simple explanations, since old boundaries have blurred and new configurations have yet to solidify.

Complicating the allocation of responsibility for adult education is the question of type: should the public sector, the individual, or the employer be held responsible for foundational skills? Who should be responsible for work-related learning? Do adults get an opportunity for liberal education? In the traditional institutional division of labor, the ideal is that the state supports general education through the public school system along with a patchwork of "second-chance" programs offering education for adults, and private employers support training that is job-specific and tailored to a particular organization.[21] This is justified in the abstract by human capital theory (Becker 1975). Differentiating between two categories of human capital, *general* and *specific,* the argument is that general skills are those foundational competencies that can be transferred from employer to employer and therefore should be underwritten by the society as a whole. Specific skills, as their name indicates, are nontransferable, and the theory argues that the firm should finance their acquisition. (This differentiation resembles the pragmatic/liberal typology.) So the employer-sponsorship of *literacy* education, literacy being among the most general of general skills, contradicts the basic tenets of human capital theory and seems to confound the existing system of funding and responsibility apportionment. Because the reality is so different than theoretically supposed, alternative explanations must be sought.

WHAT EDUCATION FOR WHOM?

Implicit in the previous discussions of purpose and responsibility is another core philosophical question, that of allocation: what education *for whom?* "You've taught them too much," I was told. I assume that "too much" related to the general information I had offered over and above the specific work skills, though I suspect that "too much" also alluded to the empowered attitude that such learning engendered. Knowledge and empowerment were not the attributes desired in "them," the lower level trainees. Why them? Why do certain people deserve less, and others more? Do some warrant liberal education and others pragmatic? If so, who decides? These are questions of social control and social justice, long evident in American discourse about education, and uniquely made manifest in the new schoolhouse.

A historical perspective offers the following: In the preindustrial era, the economic elite did not depend upon publicly funded education, so the discussion was a paternalistic debate about "them"—the masses. What the masses "needed" to learn might well differ from what the elite taught their own children, even in America; indeed, elite education at that time was very much in the Socratic tradition, a broad education "for life" carried out under religious auspices.[22] Those so chosen and educated would presumably be ready to meet whatever the future would hold. Others would play lesser roles in the democracy and in the economy, educated minimally in a pragmatic manner. This controversy took on a different tone as industrialization proceeded, and was openly debated in 1900 at a public meeting between Charles Eliot, president of Harvard University, and psychologist G. Stanley Hall of Clark University. Hall advocated a diversified curriculum that would meet the needs of all students, while Eliot desired an intellectually demanding course of studies designed to ensure excellence for those who could rise to the challenge (Grant 1988). Diversified versus demanding does not translate simply to the ideal types of liberal and pragmatic, nor to the general and specific categories of the labor economists, though at the time, the "intellectually demanding" course of study were general rather than specific, and eschewed practical applicability. This debate could also be seen in the opposing views on African American education proposed by Booker T. Washington and W.E.B. DuBois. Washington argued for practical skills for all, while DuBois advocated that a "talented tenth" receive an intellectual education to prepare them for leadership in uplifting the race. This allocation question resonates with those contradictory American beliefs about equality and individual achievement, adding the contentious issue of excellence versus equity.

The American system still struggles to reconcile these core tensions, and perpetual public education reform is one outcome. On the surface it appears that diversified (e.g., comprehensive, as well as pragmatic) and demanding (e.g., college preparatory, liberal, and broad in scope) curricula exist for youth, with a variety of structural and individual factors determining which course a particular student will "choose." Upon closer scrutiny, it can be seen that, despite the ideology of equal education for all, the system's resources are allocated disparately if not unfairly. Some students, usually the economic elites, have been relegated to the "liberal" track, while the less privileged are directed into the "pragmatic" track.[23] This is justified using the merit argument, saying that all students begin with the same opportunity, and that the more intelligent and ambitious choose to take advantage of the education offered them and deservedly become the elite.

Disparate allocation along the lines of merit or intelligence does not explain why so many adults end up in the workplace without adequate basic skills—it would seem that literacy is a prerequisite for all subsequent learning, whether liberal or pragmatic. Yet all students do not truly begin with the same opportunity, and the choices are more elusive than real, despite liberal and conservative reforms. Moreover, on an individual level, the connection between intelligence and inequality is relatively weak, challenging the merit argument.[24] Some scholars suggest that the resulting inequalities are necessary in a capitalistic society, where schools actively reproduce economic inequities and the economic system relies upon these differences in ability and ambition, despite rhetoric about equal opportunity.[25] However understood, the resulting stratification is troubling, given the cultural value of equality and overriding belief in the education solution. The unease generated by this inequity inspires not only more reform at the K-12 level but also efforts to establish a comprehensive adult remediation system, the subject of the next chapter. The debate about allocation illuminates the contradictory nature and power of the educational ideology—the system is not as fair as it purports to be, especially obvious when the problem under consideration is adult illiteracy. Such is the historical and cultural context that sets the stage for further analysis of workplace literacy programs.

Ideology and Real Consequences

In summary, there is an American propensity to believe that education will ameliorate social and economic inequities and that education can be the solution to a wide range of social problems. One consequence of this ideology is that educational goals have become overly ambitious yet full of contradictions: while expectations are high, funding is often inadequate. In the case of literacy, the private sector has taken up the slack, yet tension between private and public purposes is heightened when responsibility is differently apportioned. The purpose of education can depend upon whether learners are adults or children, and the purpose can determine whether funding comes from public, private, or individual resources. Yet questions of purpose are often submerged as the powerful ideology holds sway. By examining the purpose of education in the new schoolhouse, I attempt to see beyond beliefs to the real consequences of workplace literacy education. Yet we cannot discount this ideology—in both strength and contour, it affects the individuals involved.

Beliefs about the education solution and the fairness of American policies, however true or false, must be taken seriously. Such beliefs affect the actions and prospects of the workers, managers, educators, and owners who are all struggling to prosper in the contemporary economy. As sociologist W. I.

Thomas stated so succinctly, "If men define situations as real, they are real in their consequences." The consequences deserve attention and understanding. Chapter Two will consider the field of adult literacy in order to show the political and philosophical consequences of the education ideology when adult literacy is the topic of concern.

NOTES

1. This can be considered ideology as a way of knowing (in Mannheim's sense), rather than ideology as manipulative political posturing (Kettler et al. 1984:65). Yet politics are present—the education ideology clearly reflects a singular way of knowing, rooted in the history and culture of the Western, modern, privileged classes.

2. A classic work on this topic is *Habits of the Heart: Individualism and Commitment in American Life*, by Robert Bellah, et al. (Berkeley: University of California, 1985). This book suggests that American individualism exists in constant tension with our desires for community and connection. Robert Putnam's *Bowling Alone* buttresses the individuality argument with recent statistics and an argument for the value of social capital (New York: Simon & Schuster, 2000). Gert Hofstede, from a more analytical perspective, positions North Americans significantly higher than other peoples on a scale of individualism He links individualism with attitudes towards work and definitions of success. See *Culture's Consequences: International Differences in Work-Related Values* (Beverly Hills: Sage, 1980).

3. The United States spends more on education for children and less on social welfare than does any other industrial society, the inference being that the nation is more committed to equality of opportunity than equality of condition. This idea is developed in Steven Brint and Jerome Karabel's *The Diverted Dream: Community Colleges and the Promise of Educational Opportunity in America, 1900-1985* (New York: Oxford University Press, 1989).

4. This classical dichotomy was called to my attention in the oft-cited article by IBM executives Lewis M. Branscombe and Paul C. Gilmore titled "Education in Private Industry," *Daedalus* (Winter 1975). These authors, in turn, referenced a review by Paul McClintock of Alvin Toffler's book, *Learning for Tomorrow*, where McClintock associated Toffler with the Sophists. Further inquiry into Greek philosophy illuminated the poles of the debate, yet I hesitated to rely upon the names alone for my categorization because of the potentially confusing allusion to Socratic teaching methods. Hence my ideal types are labeled pragmatic and liberal.

5. In their *Daedalus* article, Branscombe and Gilmore articulate this tension, and conclude that colleges should keep the responsibility for liberal education themselves. However, they lament the fact that the academic communities may not share the economic interests of businesses like IBM, and fear that the university version of liberal may be just too unrealistic for business needs. While they do not reflect upon the extent to which business needs should dominate the university's mission, others certainly have taken on this question. The alternative perspective is that universities are overly defined by corporate interests, and have bowed to market forces rather than the higher goals of knowledge and wisdom. See, among others, Sheila A. Slaughter and Larry Leslie, *Academic Capitalism: Politics, Policies, and the Entrepreneurial University* (Baltimore: Johns Hopkins University Press, 1999).

6. Historian Joseph F. Kett came to this conclusion in his 1994 analysis of adult education in America, *The Pursuit of Knowledge Under Difficulty* (Stanford, CA. Stanford University Press, 1994). See Chapter Twelve, "The Learning Society" for a discussion of learners' motivations.

7. Despite the assertions of some policy makers and educators, there is no evidence that such policies result in better schooling for all, or in the diminishment of ubiquitous social problems. See Bruce Fuller and Richard F. Elmore, eds., *Who Chooses? Who Loses? Culture, Institutions, and the Unequal Effects of School Choice* (New York: Teachers College Press, 1996). The final chapter is particularly useful, as it summarizes others' empirical research.

8. Data at the organizational level are more controversial than those at the individual or national levels. Most recently, the 1999 Conference Board Report, *Turning Skills into Profit* (Bloom and Lafleur), asserted the positive relationship between training and company productivity, though conclusions are not reported quantitatively. Over the past several decades, Michael Useem has done a great deal of research and thinking on this topic, with mixed findings. For a comprehensive review of his and others' research on the relationship between skills and profit, see his chapter, "Corporate Education and Training" in *The American Corporation Today*, edited by Karl Kaysen (New York: Oxford University Press, 1996).

9. Nell Eurich describes the latter phenomenon in *Corporate Classrooms: The Learning Business* (1985) and *The Learning Industry: Education for Adult Workers* (1990). Both are published by Carnegie Foundation for the Advancement of Teaching and are available from Princeton University Press.

10. Because this book is about education for incumbent workers, my focus will not be education as an anti-poverty mechanism; however, there are parallels in the rhetoric: education is purportedly the solution for firms *and* individuals in search of economic security. For a scathing and empirically convincing critique of the use of job training to attempt to alleviate urban poverty, see Gordon Lafer, "The Politics of Job Training," *Politics and Society* 22, no. 3 (Summer 1994): 349-388.

11. These efforts were summarized and critiqued in an article by labor economists Mun C. Tsang, Russell W. Rumberger, and Henry M. Levin, "The Impact of Surplus Schooling on Worker Productivity," *Industrial Relations* 30, no. 2 (1991): 209-228. Richard Rubinson and Irene Browne reviewed the work/education link from a sociological perspective in chapter 23 of the *Handbook of Economic Sociology*, edited by Neil J. Smelser and Richard Swedberg (Princeton, NJ: Princeton University Press, 1994). They stated simply, "The earlier, common assumption that education is the key to both individual economic advancement and national economic growth and development has been challenged by much sociological research" (581). They spent a significant portion of the chapter tracing the basis of the assumption, and reviewing the multiple efforts at proving and debunking. Most recently, the complex relationships among the educational requirements of jobs, the educational levels of the labor force, and growing wage inequality have been explored by Frederic L. Pryor and David L. Schaffer, *Who's Not Working and Why: Employment, Cognitive Skills, Wages and the Changing U.S. Labor Market* (New York: Cambridge University Press, 1999).

12. Ivar Berg set the overeducation debate in motion in *Education and Jobs: The Great Training Robbery* (New York: Praeger, 1970). His arguments have been regularly updated—see bibliographic references for Rumberger (1981); Tsang Rumberger and Levin (1991); Marcotte (1999); Pryor and Schaffer (1999); and Sum (1999). A "basic

skills surplus" is documented in a Hudson Institute report entitled *Workforce 2020* (Judy, D'Amico, and Bernstein 1997). Curiously, the concept of overeducation has never gained wide acceptance among popular audiences or educators, perhaps because it so strongly contradicts the ideology of the education-solution. *Over*education is an oxymoron to the educator who holds unlimited individual development as an unstated goal; furthermore, it is problematic for those who think that the purpose of education is more than just to prepare for the workplace.

13. For a thorough, if atheoretical, review of the U.S. literature on new forms of work organization, see *Change at Work,* Cappelli et al. (1997). Vicki Smith's review essay, "New Forms of Work Organization," in the 1997 *Annual Review of Sociology* 23: 315-339, describes the "flatly confusing" consequences of what she refers to as the flexible model. "High performance" became a common term used to contrast the new with the traditional, even though a 1995 Census Bureau survey found that, "Despite the considerable attention given to the new modes of work organization, the use of high-performance work systems remains the exception rather than the rule." Cited in William H. Miller, "The Future? Not Yet," *Industry Week* (April 17, 1995): 73. With regard to the learning organization concept, the management literature features voluminous exemplars. Peter Senge may be best known for his various works on the learning organization, starting with *The Fifth Discipline: The Art and Practice of the Learning Organization* (New York: Doubleday, 1990).

14. Anyone that has been writing about work or organizations over the past decade has taken up the topic of changing skill requirements, though findings are far from definitive and are complicated by the fact that the definition of skill is itself controversial. Michael Useem offers a thoughtful overview in his 1996 chapter in Kaysen's *The American Corporation Today*. Less critical, but more up to date is the research cited in the National Organizations study (Kalleberg, et al., *Organizations in America*, 1996). These assertions about changing skill have earned an acronym, FWSL (future work skills literature), and have engendered significant critique (see note below).

15. There is an optimistic discussion of intellective skills and their potential impact on the organization of work in Shoshana Zuboff's *In the Age of the Smart Machine: The Future of Work and Power* (New York: Basic Books, 1988). A more critical, earlier assessment of the relationship between computer-mediated work, employee autonomy, and social inequality is provided by Robert Howard in *Brave New Workplace* (New York: Penguin, 1985). In *Power in the Workplace* Steven Vallas offers a useful theoretical overview of the technology/labor process control debate (second chapter), coupled with an empirical perspective that concludes that technology has been given such power as to separate the concerns about worker skill from those of managerial control (Albany: SUNY Press, 1993).

16. Scholars in various disciplines have written about work attitudes "needed," and this has been the subject of government studies. A report from the National Center for Research in Vocational Education, written by Cathleen Stasz and Dominic J. Brewer, *Academic Skills at Work, Two Perspectives* (MDS-1193) (Berkeley: National Center for Research in Vocational Education, 1999) reviews the literature and reiterates the employers' concern about soft skills and attitudes rather than technical knowledge. From the management perspective, Peter Cappelli has written on the primacy of work attitudes over work skills. See especially his 1995 piece, "Rethinking the 'Skills Gap,' " in *California Management Review* 37, no 4: 108-124. Robert Reich pushed for investment in training and education in *The Work of Nations* (New York: A. A. Knopf, 1991). He

popularized the idea of the American worker as symbolic analyst, also writing about attitudinal attributes. The "SCANS Report," also 1991, was quite influential. See *What Work Requires of Schools: A SCANS Report for America 2000* by Secretary's Commission on Achieving Necessary Skills (Washington, DC: U.S. Department of Labor, 1991). Also, James O'Toole offered a much earlier analysis in his book, *Work, Learning, and the American Future* (San Francisco: Jossey-Bass, 1977).

17. Vicky Smith includes the research on the intensification of work demands in her review of the literature on flexibility, "New Forms of Work Organization" (1997). See note 12 above.

18. Debate on this topic takes the form of a literature rather than a single theory, and anthropologist Charles Darrah devised the acronym FWSL—future work skills literature—to capture the substance of the concerns. See *Learning and Work: An Exploration in Industrial Ethnography* (New York: Garland, 1996). The FWSL has the following ideas at its core: in the new knowledge-based economy, brains have seemingly replaced brawn as the technique of production, and great attention is being given to the cognitive demands of work. "High performance workplaces" increasingly look to non-managers to make decisions and rely upon teams to perform job tasks, so the communicative demands on lower level workers have changed as well. The mainstream branch of the FWSL literature is evident in the SCANS report, cited above. Also, Anthony Carnevale and colleagues wrote several volumes, defining skill noncritically. See *Workplace Basics* (San Francisco: Jossey-Bass, 1990) and *The Learning Enterprise* (Washington, DC: The American Society for Training and Development and the U.S. Department of Labor, 1989). Darrah, along with others, takes a critical perspective, and argues that technical and attitudinal skills cannot be taken out of context, and suggests that to understand the demands of the workplace, it is necessary to observe groups of workers doing their job tasks. Context is important, argue researchers who assert that "high levels of training have little effect unless matched to high performance productive systems." See Peter Cappelli and Nikolai Rogovsky, "New Work Systems and Skill Requirements," *International Labour Review* 133, no. 2 (1994): 211.

19. According to *Business Week Special Report* (April 20, 1987), the U.S. could boast that 50% of high school graduates go to college, but only 70% of students finish high school, as opposed to Japan, where 98% complete high school. MIT's Lester Thurow concluded, "Their bottom half is beating our bottom half." Comparisons on standardized math and reading tests also revealed that the U.S. was behind other industrialized nations. On the college level, a shortage of engineers, scientists, and manufacturing experts was predicted, along with a loss of skilled teachers in these fields. More than a decade hence, statistics are similar, though the Japanese "miracle" has been discredited.

20. The public/private distinction can be misleading here, since private schools have always existed in the U.S., and provide a choice for those who wish an alternative to the publicly funded education system. In keeping with American values, the decision to attend public or private school is an individual choice, made by children and their families, and is largely determined by family wealth and religious orientation.

21. The training system is far from consolidated, and includes significant overlap among private and public, and between general and specific skills. The following chart attempts to outline the landscape:

Institutions	Source of support	Target audience	Type of education
elementary and secondary schools	largely public	youth	general; vocational
colleges and universities	public, private, individual	young adult, adult	general, professional, vocational (community colleges)
post-secondary occupational education	public, private, individual	the 50% of youth who do not go on to college	occupation specific
apprenticeship programs	labor unions	young adults	occupational training
second chance training	federal and state government	disadvantaged and dislocated populations	remedial and occupational
career support system	employers	incumbent workers	firm specific; employability
training industry/ consultants	employers, individuals	educators and trainers	job-specific
employer-based training and development	employers	new and incumbent workers	job-specific, firm-specific, developmental, professional

22. These (and subsequent) critical ideas about the history of education in America are derived from the work of Michael Katz, *Reconstructing American Education* (Cambridge: Harvard University Press, 1987).

23. I do not do justice here to the complexity of this debate, documented thoroughly by numerous scholars in the field. The Katz book cited above provides a useful beginning. However, it is worth noting that professional education is just one of the aspects of the system that confound this generalization. Elites attend law school and medical school—usually tickets to high status, yet overwhelming in their practical approach to the education task.

24. See, among others, *Meritocracy and Economic Inequality*, edited by Kenneth Arrow, Samuel Bowles, and Steven Durlauf (Princeton NJ: Princeton University Press, 2000).

25. The influential and controversial classic *Schooling in Capitalist America*, written by Samuel Bowles and Herbert Gintis (New York: Basic Books, 1976), argued that the U.S. educational system primarily corresponded with the needs of the private sector employers. School structure is thought to reflect the needs of the capitalistic work system, and work attitudes learned through years of schooling are as important as cognitive skills. Passive workers with low expectations fill the bottom tier jobs, more thoughtful workers become middle managers, and highly (liberally) educated free-thinkers are those who take control and reap the greatest rewards. Different types of secondary school

experiences thus correspond with occupational achievement and economic success. This process by which education reproduces inequality while purporting to do otherwise has also been theorized by European scholars of education and society: Pierre Bourdieu and Jean-Claude Passeron wrote the widely cited *Reproduction in Education, Society, and Culture,* translated by Richard Nice (Beverly Hills: Sage, 1977).

2

The Policies, Politics, and Philosophies of Literacy Education

The cherished beliefs about the importance of education in American culture are severely tested by the existence of significant numbers of adults who are illiterate. According to the National Institute for Literacy (NIFL), in 1999 about 40 million American adults were without a high school credential, and at least 6 million lacked English skills. Only about 5 million are thought to be truly illiterate, that is, not able to read and write at all, though approximately 22% of the adult population tested in the lowest quintile of a recent standardized exam.[1] Employers are decidedly affected by illiteracy, since the majority of illiterate adults are in the workforce. The U.S. Department of Labor places illiteracy's costs to businesses at about $225 billion per annum. The costs result from employee mistakes, injuries, absenteeism, tardiness, and missed opportunities. Illiteracy is a problem for which education is an obvious solution, yet the policy response has been inadequate. Business involvement in literacy education appears to compensate for the lack of public resources, though this has created additional tensions, and raises several questions.

- What is the nature of private sector involvement in literacy policy?
- What are the political, cultural, and historical contexts in which employer-sponsored literacy programs have been instituted?
- Who are the chief advocates for illiterate adults, and what are their attitudes towards employer sponsorship?
- How do the professionalization efforts of those in the adult literacy field affect workplace literacy programs?

The previous chapter suggested that adults in need of basic skills education are somehow at odds with cultural beliefs about who deserves educational opportunity. This conflict is played out in the ideological debates about purpose and responsibility. This chapter will build upon the discussion of ideology to show the ways in which the adult literacy field negotiates employer involvement in the literacy "crisis." The fragmented nature of U.S. literacy policy, the radical and pragmatic politics surrounding the provision of literacy, and the movement-like tenor of the adult education field will be described in order to allow better understanding of the consequences of employer sponsorship.

THE PIECES OF LITERACY POLICY

Illiterate adults are a diverse group—ranging from those who were school failures because of learning disabilities, to those who know the mechanics of reading and writing but are seemingly lacking higher order thinking skills or desired work attitudes, to immigrants without formal education even in their native language. What they share are several barriers to attaining the education they need. There is a stigma associated with illiteracy in American culture, and thus one obstacle to provision of adult compensatory education is getting the student to publicly admit his or her need. This is less true for the non-English-speaking students, especially if they have newly arrived in the U.S., yet it is still a factor. Once students have made it to the educational setting, they are usually highly motivated, for a range of reasons: family, religion, and work all contribute to the process whereby an adult will ask for help. This self-motivation makes the adult classroom markedly different than children's classrooms, as will be elaborated upon further.

The second barrier, perhaps more significant than the first, is funding. Of the 40 million to 44 million adults with literacy needs, only about 4 million (10%) are enrolled in educational programs, according to the U.S. Department of Education. The enrollment breakdown is as follows (1998 data):[2]

Adult Basic Education (ABE) (below eighth grade skills level)	38%
Adult Secondary Education (eighth–twelfth grade skill level)	23%
English as a Second Language (ESL or ESOL)	39%

There are waiting lists for nearly all community-based programs, and classes can be crowded and materials scarce. This shortage is addressed by a patchwork of policy solutions, involving the public sector, volunteers, and labor unions, in addition to employers.

State and Federal Solutions

The federal government funds an array of service, research, and technical assistance programs for adult education. States manage the programmatic aspects, and get much of their funding from national sources, occasionally supplemented by local appropriations. Funding from all sources is erratic, though increasing at a steady rate. Federal money for adult literacy doubled from 1980 to 1990, and again from 1997 to 2000. Expenditures will reach an all-time high in 2000, at nearly $900 million (*NIFL Policy Update*, November 19, 1999).

Pressure from employers has played a prominent role in this increased allocation and in the creation of a permanent federal agency to support adult literacy. The National Literacy Act (NLA) was passed in 1991, after a decade of effort. Success of this legislation was in part due to the active private sector lobby, with the Business Council for Effective Literacy (now defunct) playing a central role. Their influence is evident in the language of the law, as well as in the governance structures. The mandate of the NLA is, "To enhance the literacy and basic skills of adults, to ensure that all adults in the United States acquire the basic skills necessary to function effectively and achieve the greatest possible opportunity in their work and in their lives, and to strengthen and coordinate adult literacy programs."[3] This federal legislation also created and funded a new independent National Institute for Literacy (NIFL), an intergovernmental agency spanning the Departments of Education, Labor, and Health and Human Services. Notably, the NIFL has a board of directors that includes the private/not-for profit sectors and adult learners. This board composition is representative of its philosophy: by assuring that employers, educators, organized labor, and students themselves be given a voice, the NIFL enacts its belief that literacy policy is everyone's concern. Work, family, and community participation are the recurrent themes.

The emphasis given to business interests, coupled with the inevitable acknowledgment that literacy education in the workplace may benefit employers more than employees, continues to be controversial. Longstanding tensions between educators and employers have been played out in the public arena, as the Departments of Labor and Education struggle with each other for jurisdiction over adult education funds, with the ostensible difference being their definitions of the purpose of such education. The fear is that employers (represented by the Department of Labor) will construe literacy narrowly, to what is needed for work, and that educators will construe literacy so broadly as to be of minimal usefulness in helping illiterate adults obtain gainful employment. (The Department of Labor also is supposed to represent employee interests, but their view of people-as-workers is criticized for being unduly constrained.) The Department of Education argues that their agency is best able to maintain a broader definition of purpose, not limited to preparation for employment, and thereby to design programs appropriate for adults. Labor, on the other hand, takes the perspective that work is the necessary pragmatic outcome, not denying that basic literacy may well have benefits beyond the workplace. One outcome of this disagreement has been a fragmented funding stream, with both agencies (among occasional others) allocating money to literacy, though none adequately.

Public funding for workplace-based literacy programs is another outcome of the disagreement: here, the work-versus-education conflict was addressed by requiring a collaborative model of workplace literacy education.[4] Grants were typically awarded to educational agencies that formed partnerships with groups of employers and/or unions, though occasionally corporations were the direct recipients. Fueled by the late 1980s' rhetoric about crises in competitiveness and in education, the federal government began the Workplace Literacy Initiative, designed to provide financial support and demonstrate effective models. Between 1988 and 1991, slightly more than 200 grants were made, totaling $60 million. While the early money went to large companies for short durations (twelve to eighteen months), the program was modified in 1991 to favor small businesses and to allow longer programs (up to three years).[5] In FY93, $18.9 million was allocated, down $0.5 million from the previous year. Decreases in federal support continued, and federal workplace funding ended in 1995.[6]

There is no evidence that the state or federal government funded such corporate-based general education efforts in prior eras, so, from the policy perspective, workplace literacy was considered a "new field" in 1991.[7] Yet this new field was short lived. That public support was discontinued reflects the fragmented and politicized nature of the literacy system as much as government interests in privatizing this responsibility. The Workplace Literacy Initiative funds were explicitly conceived of as providing "seed money," with a required percentage of employer financing. The goal was for employers to fully fund these literacy efforts, and to serve as models for other employers. Approximately 20% of employers continue to support literacy classes for their workers, a significant investment, but not nearly the comprehensive policy solution that was envisioned.

Volunteer and Labor Solutions

Fortunately for those adults seeking to improve their literacy, such education does not rely upon public sector funding. Volunteers and labor unions have been important providers. For many years, volunteers were responsible for most adult compensatory education, and they still offer a significant and largely unheralded amount of teaching. Volunteers are typically affiliated with two major voluntary literacy organizations: Literacy Volunteers of America (LVA) and Laubach Literacy Action. LVA and Laubach serve the most challenging segment of the adult learning population—persons with the lowest skills, lower than most existing adult basic education or ESL programs can handle. The volunteers primarily provide one-on-one tutoring, with the occasional formal group instruction programs. Typically run out of libraries, churches and community centers, these services are occasionally based in workplaces.

In the past decade, organized labor has drawn increased attention to basic skills and literacy, no doubt responding to the prevalent competitiveness rhetoric as well as attempting to define a new relevancy for itself in the face of declining numbers and influence. Nearly all of the federal and state funders require labor involvement if the workplace is unionized. At the same time, unions have received direct public funds for literacy and have been in the forefront of efforts to assure that technical skills training is preceded and/or accompanied by the necessary instruction in reading and math. Typically such courses are community based, or conducted in union halls rather than in workplaces, though the requirement of union membership limits their enrollment. In highly union-

ized organizations, labor has had an active role in creating and perpetuating onsite literacy programs even without other public sector funding.[8]

Statistics for direct or indirect labor involvement in the provision of literacy are difficult to come by because of the collaborative model and the fact
that in certain cases labor may bargain for employer support of such programs,
and therefore be instrumental in their implementation, but may not offer funding
or other oversight. Several decades past, unions were a significant educational
resource, offering basic skills and citizenship education as well as critical labor
literacy.[9] Now that labor strength is diminished, employers may be taking on
this responsibility (with less attention to radical labor interests, of course). Some
feel that unions should return to a stronger educative role in order to counter the
negative effects of corporate involvement in education, while others take the
pragmatic approach that all resources are welcome, whatever the source.[10]

Even taken collectively, these approaches result in a fragmented and
incomplete system of literacy education. The barriers persist: stigma and lack of
resources are only slightly mitigated by recent efforts to institutionalize and consolidate national programs. No sector has a clear mandate for solving the illiteracy problem, and politics presents a third barrier. Government leaders are hesi-
tant about the extent of their commitment to a group of adults who apparently
squandered the educational opportunities offered them as youth, and politicians
also resist full-scale commitment to immigrant education because of the anti-
immigrant temper of the times. Employers want to train in work skills, not basic
reading and writing. Volunteers have little visibility and episodic tolerance for
the politics of the issue. Labor unions represent only a fraction of the illiterate
adults, and have more pressing global concerns. The adults themselves, unor-
ganized with limited English proficiency, are hardly a powerful constituency.
Adult educators have emerged as the champions of illiterate adults and literacy
education, yet they must operate in a remarkably politicized environment.

ADULT EDUCATION PHILOSOPHY AND METHODS

The field of adult education has politics at its core. Adult education, defined as providing foundational skills for adults, thus not including enrichment
and job-related learning, is a field "normatively strong even though structurally
and financially weak, as much a movement as a service" (Squires 1992:88).
These norms revolve around the philosophy that adult learning should bring
about personal liberation, and that teaching methods should be participatory or
"learner-centered." The field attracts those who are disillusioned by the politics
and rigidity of the traditional educational system, yet who see themselves as
providing a much-needed service to a population that has been marginalized.
The movement has several branches, the most powerful of which can be considered Freirian, referring to the critical consciousness advocated by Brazilian educator and activist Paolo Freire. Freirian philosophy takes the stance that since
illiterate adults are often economically and politically disempowered, adult education must be designed to bring about emancipation as much as basic skill acquisition.[11] Emancipation is political and personal, with the goal of education

being to become more fully human, an end aligned with the Socratic tradition discussed in Chapter One. Freire's belief that radical social change can be brought about through participatory adult education is appealing to frustrated social movement actors, as well as to those discouraged by the persistent inequities in the U.S. public education system for youth. Those on this extreme end of the movement, are, not surprisingly, disparaging of "those who would simply make schools an adjunct of the corporation or the workplace."[12]

Another prominent branch of the movement is "andragogy," that is, the science of educating adults. Andragogy is contrasted with pedagogy, teaching methods for children. As popularized by Malcolm Knowles in Britain during the late 1960s, and by Steven Brookfield in the United States during the 1980s, this is a philosophy of participatory, self-directed learning, with the teacher serving to facilitate, not lead, and the educational goal being individual growth, empowerment, and emancipation. Adults are not "taught," rather, they are "helped to learn." Learner-centered goals are assumed to be liberatory rather than simply work-related, though adult students have been known to disappoint their teachers, simply in search of the credential or skill-set needed to get a raise.

Many adult educators espouse a participatory philosophy and learner-centered methods, whether or not they use the term *andragogy*. They may embrace this philosophy and method because it advocates radical change in power relationships, along the lines of Paolo Freire, or because they think that the learning theory is sound, based as it is in cognitive psychology. The participatory philosophy is visible in classroom practices, program designs, and public policy mandates, a fact that is important to understanding employer oversight of workplace literacy programs. The adult educators use their unique (and quietly oppositional) philosophy and their movement-inspired energy to influence the way in which literacy is taught in the workplace. The policy debates about purpose and allocation become esoteric once teachers close the classroom door. They are given this autonomy because of their professional status, a still evolving development.

THE PROFESSIONAL PROJECT IN THE WORKPLACE

Adult educators have had to differentiate and legitimize their expertise in order to establish the professional identity, necessary in the contemporary occupational environment. Like others in professionalizing occupations, adult educators seek the professional label and its accompanying power for several reasons: to influence policy decisions, to receive greater social respect, and to assure more secure and lucrative employment.[13] Though professionalization is not universally sought after by practitioners in the field, tenuous working conditions alone offer compelling reasons to seek improvement in status, pay, and power. Most teachers are not full-time employees of any organization, but are hired on a contract basis as need and resources warrant. Often working for several programs at the same time, they are paid hourly, and rarely have benefits or job security beyond the semester or the grant cycle. Yet, despite the low pay and status, many adult educators have a master's degree or post-baccalaureate training in adult learning. Two comparison groups are college teachers and industry trainers, both of whom enjoy more favorable working conditions and greater respect than do adult literacy educators. Along the same lines, those who teach children have job security and political clout, in part because of their union affiliation.

Professionalization may have been hindered in its early stages by the perception that the adult education field is a movement populated by former 1960s radicals and ideological church groups, but practitioners have since learned to use their philosophical beliefs as a symbol of uniqueness and expertise. Nonetheless, there is resistance within the ranks, since professionalization is an inherently conservative process, but this resistance is tempered by the pragmatic desire to gain resources and the realization that the adult educators will not necessarily give up their ideals, even if they choose to work in employer-sponsored programs.

Consequently, it appears that the professionalization project has accelerated of late, with the adult education field consolidating and gaining a national office, and the nation as a whole becoming committed to "lifelong learning" and a "learning society" (Kett 1994). Two key factors determine if an occupation is to achieve professional status and influence organizational dynamics: one, a knowledge base grounded in university recognized expertise, and two, professional networks.[14] Both are increasingly apparent among adult educators. The knowledge base of the field has been steadily developing, in adult education as a whole and in the subspecialties of second-language acquisition and workplace learning. Universities and colleges now allow undergraduates and graduate students to major in adult education and/or ESOL, and a master's degree is often a prerequisite for employment. At the same time, a great deal of in-service education is available for adult educators, through a system of professional development linked to the community college systems in various states. Federal literacy allocations include sums for staff development.[15] Depending upon the type of program in which they work, adult education professionals are required and/or paid to attend ongoing education courses in their field. In such formal learning settings, there is an attempt to connect the practice of adult teaching to the cognitive theories of andragogy and to theories of adult development. This knowledge building is an especially crucial aspect of the professionalization project.

The second mechanism, the professional network, has increased in size and stature, contributing to the development of specific expertise and encouraging its dissemination. On the global level, the internet has enhanced professional communication and networking possibilities among adult educators and scholars in the field. Several list serves have been organized, and postings range from questions about citizenship curriculum, to teaching English to Somali immigrants, to the latest research findings in cognitive science. Networking happens in the traditional manner as well. The Massachusetts Coalition of Adult Educators (MCAE) is an active association that is strongly affiliated with the Division of Adult Education within the State Department of Education, and has linkages with the long-established Massachusetts Manufacturers Association. MCAE employs a full time association director, and sponsors a yearly conference, called "Network," with sessions devoted to a range of professional concerns. There are informal networks as well, usually regional in character, that assist in the employment process and indirectly influence the activities and beliefs of the adult educators. Through shared employers, attendance at meetings, and involvement in workshops, the informal network professionalizes the occupation by affirming similar experiences, allowing teachers a forum in which to discuss student concerns, and developing a sense of collegial practice. From each other, teachers learn who the "good" employers are, which funding sources are waxing and waning, and what development activities are useful and lucrative.

Along with the knowledge base and associational mechanisms, a third factor should be considered as professionalization progresses: social trusteeship. Traditionally, professionals in a society were thought to have a moral responsibility to use their knowledge for the good of the community. This aspect of professionalism is on the wane, as expertise for personal and organizational benefit has become the norm,[16] but adult literacy educators can be considered an exception. Social responsibility is at the heart of the adult education field, as shown by the description of philosophy and methods, and these educators' political orientation is often more radical than that of other social welfare professionals. Given professional status or not, this group will likely continue to challenge the status quo on behalf of the oppressed, and will continue to define education as raising consciousness as well as teaching skills. Practitioners in the field are inspired and sustained by this sense of contributing to the greater good, and it has served to create their unique identity. This identity becomes especially important when adult educators bring their expertise and beliefs to settings that are not necessarily hospitable to critical consciousness—like the workplace.

Ironically, literacy education offered in the workplace, as opposed to the traditional community or school setting, enhances their professionalization project. Adult educators, in search of identity and legitimacy in their own field, cannot afford to completely acquiesce to corporate goals, yet must convince employers that corporate interests will be served by hiring a literacy specialist.[17] At the same time, teachers who work in firms rather than schools must be able to differentiate their goals from those of the organization. To do so requires that they defend their professional expertise, thus advancing their professionalization project. Furthermore, adult educators must differentiate themselves from the trainers and organizational development professionals employed by the firm if they are to assure continued employment.[18] As a result, adult educators have convinced the employers that teaching literacy requires expertise, thereby increasing the demand for their professional services at the same time as they improve their status. Along the same lines, a few teachers have been successful in attaining full time positions for themselves as employees of the organization that first hired them on a contract basis to teach a few hours a week. While some may accuse these educators of "selling out," in general, full time employment in a literacy position is a badge of legitimacy for the field, given even more value in the current political environment by the fact that the private sector deems such expertise worth supporting.

In the new schoolhouse, the teachers' professional status potentially allows them significant influence with regard to teaching methods and program design. (This is an empirical issue, to be elaborated upon in Chapter Four.) However, because the teachers are not managers and usually not even employed directly by the firm, they may not be able to influence organizational dynamics beyond their classrooms. The social trusteeship aspect of their professional identity is not powerful enough to overcome organizational expectations, even as it allows them to differentiate themselves from trainers and other organizational professionals. Does their emerging professional status translate to political influence on the national level, as the social trusteeship label implies? To a certain extent. As a group, they have been stymied by the longstanding politics surrounding adult literacy. [19]

THE POLITICS OF LITERACY

On the surface, literacy politics are a puzzle: the U.S. values education highly, yet consistently underfunds the education of adults. Less wealthy, less developed nations have higher literacy rates than the U.S., so the problem cannot be attributed to economics.[20] Understanding of cognitive development, learning styles, and special populations has mushroomed in the past several decades, so educational technique cannot be blamed. Although illiterate adults are a powerless constituency, literacy issues receive public attention and generate bipartisan support. Yet the National Institute for Literacy must continue to struggle for resources, and many adults are on waiting lists for service. Supply does not meet demand, even with the assistance of private, voluntary, and labor sectors. This underfunding may itself be a policy decision—scarcity increases the value accorded to literacy at the same time as it provides evidence that the government alone cannot adequately address what are essentially poor people's issues. I suggest that the puzzling nature of literacy politics *protects* certain interests in the national debate about poverty, immigration, education, and work. A historical constructivist perspective on literacy definitions and literacy education offers evidence.

From the constructivist perspective, there are dual considerations: the actual literacy levels of the adults under scrutiny, and the societal debate that transforms literacy from an "issue" into a "problem" into a "crisis," then frames it as intrinsically linked with other national concerns.[21] For over a century, literacy levels have steadily risen, along with median levels of schooling.[22] Still, the perception of a literacy crisis exists. The definition of literacy should then be considered variable, reflecting the norms in a given society at a given time. In the early days of the industrial revolution, writing one's name and doing basic addition were thought to characterize a literate person; at mid-century, the expectation was that the literate person could read at a fairly sophisticated level, and do complex math; and current expectations for literacy sometimes go so far as to include not just reading and writing, but using the information in a way that requires the ability to analyze and synthesize, to question assumptions and dispute arguments. Expectations have evolved over the past century, with the explanation being that the definition of literacy must keep up with increases in technology and reflect a knowledge-intensive society. Moreover, context matters: an individual may be able to function in a work setting and so be considered literate, but may be illiterate when it comes to children's homework or the pharmacy.

This explanation is challenged by consideration of literacy as a "set of cultural practices" rather than a set of skills, and consequently as an expression of power relations rather than abstract truths.[23] To illustrate, there have been eras when teaching reading was a crime. Various groups have had their access to such teaching limited: women's education was long prohibited in some parts of the world; the Tories didn't want an educated working class in the last century; in the United States it was illegal to teach slaves to read and write. Sometimes the discrimination was not codified or direct, but existed *de facto*—for example, during the 1850s in Massachusetts and Connecticut, voting rights were only granted to those who were literate, implicitly discriminating against the Irish and Catholics. Thus the decision about who is and is not "literate" reflects societal norms including long-standing power inequities.[24]

Also variable and culturally determined are the literacy "crises" that recurrently erupt, attributed in each era to different societal concerns. "Literacy as a moral imperative" in the nineteenth century shifted to "literacy for citizenship" in the early part of the twentieth century, to "literacy for work" in the current controversial conceptualization.[25] Furthermore, whenever the literacy crisis rhetoric surfaces, it is assumed that "usually something else [is] going on in the society."[26] In the contemporary era, that "something else" may be understood as being related to economic security, given the emphasis on employment. The growing polarization of incomes could be a significant factor. It is also possible that the current "crisis" is related to the foreign-born percentage of the population, now estimated to be one in ten, the highest ratio in over a hundred years. The influx of immigrants and the increasing gap between rich and poor both have the potential to upset existing power relations, so the crisis may be the challenge to the status quo, rather than any particular group's reading ability.

This is not to invalidate the statistics set forth at the beginning of the chapter, nor to imply that current literacy efforts are for naught. Rather, the constructivist rhetoric allows us to see beyond the simple explanations and the ideological gloss: perhaps literacy education does not get the attention it deserves because the nation remains ambivalent about what is owed to those who are poor and foreign born. Likewise, if literacy is defined as "for work" there is the expectation that these groups will contribute to the system, rather than become dependent. At the same time, if the literacy bar is raised ever higher, the system can continue to keep a group at the bottom. Deeming those at the bottom as "illiterate" is more politically acceptable than using ascribed characteristics such as gender or race, even though these characteristics may still predominate. Variably defined, literacy and the occasional literacy crisis can serve a range of social functions. Though literacy politics seems less of a puzzle in this context, questions remain.

How is workplace literacy education explained by suggesting that the definition of literacy is variable, and that the literacy crisis may be socially constructed? This analysis reveals that we must look below surface rhetoric regarding skills and competitiveness in order to answer the questions "why literacy?" and "why now?" Placing employer-sponsored literacy education in historical perspective will allow insight into the ways in which cultural context and social policy have been (and continue to be) intertwined.

THE HISTORY OF EMPLOYER-SPONSORED LITERACY EDUCATION

Employer involvement in literacy education is not new, despite its recent "discovery" by policy advocates. Formal basic skills education at work has occurred for nearly a century, as have controversies surrounding this private involvement in a public good. Even though these efforts were funded solely by employers, social (rather than economic) goals have typically provided justification, and skill enhancement has nearly always been accompanied by desire for attitudinal changes among workers. "Company schools" existed as early as 1913, with the goal of training employees in English, math, science, and citizenship (Fisher, 1967). A sufficient number of firms were involved to warrant the formation of an association, the National Association of Corporation Schools, comprised of the large companies of the era. While these company schools initially focused on college graduates and skilled technical workers, they soon added courses for immigrants and those public school attendees who were considered deficient or illiterate. For unskilled workers, "programs aimed at their Americanization, rather than the direct upgrading of their skills," wrote historian Bernice Fisher (1967:110-111). She went on to say that "large firms ran what were virtually elementary schools, offering English, citizenship, math, and science" (113). This was needed, according to association publications, "to make these workers efficient." Business owners eventually resisted this responsibility, arguing that basic education was more appropriately the role of the public schools. Yet they argued that public schools should change to more effectively meet industry needs by providing "solid and industrially oriented fundamental education." This sentiment gave rise to federal funding for vocational schools, codified in the Smith-Hughes bill of 1917.

For the next thirty years, employers continued to try to externalize the costs of education and training, and federal expenditures on vocational and occupational education increased. World War II changed this, as rapid economic growth coupled with an explosion of technological innovation resulted in renewed attention to in-house education and training. The post-war period was a time of great economic expansion for the U.S., and the labor supply could barely meet demand. Corporations reinstituted formal schooling, to such an extent that in 1975 U.S. Secretary of Labor John Dunlop warned of the "problem" of employer-sponsored education. He coined the term "shadow system of education" to describe the state's concern with private sector responsibility and domain.[27] In 1977, the Conference Board reported that 11% of companies offered remedial education, with 70% offering some kind of formal training. The Conference Board stated that corporate involvement in basic skills education was needed in order for companies to meet affirmative action goals, with companies again asserting that the public schools were not adequately preparing future workers. The affirmative action explanation can be understood as an alternative framing of the immigrant concerns from the early part of the century, though during this time the goals were primarily social. The debates about public versus private responsibility waxed and waned (Dunlop never generating much response to his concerns), while the shadow system grew and began to institutionalize (Scott and Meyer 1991).

Into the 1980s, companies continued to offer all sorts of training, including compensatory education. Given the tenor of the times, though, social goals were no longer the explicit justification. According to a 1985 Conference Board study, technological change and workplace reorganization were the main forces driving an overall increase in corporate training expenditures, as production lines gave way to information-intensive work, with greater expectations that employees participate in decision-making. These expectations impelled companies to offer classes in communication skills, and to rely upon formal education to assist employees with their increased responsibilities. Also fueling the training investments were the demographic characteristics of the labor force entrants. Immigrants accounted for 22% of the labor force growth between 1980 and 1987—more than twice their contribution during the 1970s when baby boomers and women entered the labor market in large numbers.[28] While a higher proportion of this wave of immigrants had attended college than people who were born in the U.S., roughly one-third had only an elementary school education, and many spoke no English at all. Yet they were potentially valuable employees— willing to take low-prestige, low-wage jobs that native-born Americans had come to refuse. Consequently, many employers increased their involvement in ESOL, and government funding for basic literacy grew, though public policy barely acknowledged that immigrants were the primary recipients.[29] Criticism of the public school system heightened, and businesses became involved in education reform at the state and federal level. The national "crisis" of economic competitiveness made it imperative that private and public sectors work together to improve educational achievement at all levels, so the debate about responsibility became less conflictual and more partnership-oriented. Education (primarily job training) in the workplace became taken for granted during this period, stabilizing the foundation of the new schoolhouse.

Looking back, it is evident that U.S. employers have called upon various explanations for their involvement in literacy education: Americanization, affirmative action, and technology. These reasons reflected changing social circumstances and beliefs about the national interest. Rarely did employers simply want to have employees who could read and write; instead, attitudinal and cultural adaptations were what the classes were supposed to accomplish, along with a modicum of basic skills enhancement. Moreover, such practices have endured consistent tensions regarding the extent of private versus public responsibility, and it appears that the boundaries between the two sectors have never been all that clear: despite rhetorical resistance, businesses have supported public policy goals such as citizenship, and the government has been involved in education that benefits a particular industry or firm.

Thus literacy education serves a variety of purposes in a given society at a given time, some of these purposes acknowledged and others less obvious. Its persistence over many decades suggests that these purposes are important, although still largely unexamined. The fact that the history of workplace education is so little known further suggests that the social constructivist argument be given credence. The current "crisis" must be viewed skeptically, yet at the same time efforts must be made to assure that literacy education is available for those who lack basic skills, since, real or constructed, basic skills are considered a necessity in contemporary life.

THE PROMISE OF WORKPLACE LITERACY

One consequence of the fragmentation of public funding for literacy education and the puzzling politicization of the issue is that an adult in need of basic skills or English language education does not find the system easy to access. Such an individual cannot simply go to a centralized agency to find out about classes available, since the local service provider may be a library, high school, church, or the employment office, depending upon any number of factors in the community. This, combined with the fact that illiteracy is already stigmatized, adds to the numbers of adults that are not getting the education they need or desire. Outreach efforts are difficult, too, because the target audience itself is dispersed, hidden in communities or workplaces, often unable to access services precisely because they lack literacy (a poster in a clinic or library would likely be unreadable). This is complicated by the scarcity of public funding for education, despite the belief in education-as-solution, and exacerbated by the fact that in the current policy environment, public funding for social services of all types is threatened. Therefore, literacy advocates have had to be relentless and inventive in finding resources to fund programs that are effective, affordable, and respectful of adult concerns.

To a certain extent, workplace literacy programs overcome the funding and outreach obstacles, primarily because the target audience is in a single location, and employers have resources in place to provide training and education. Yet this solution is by no means universally embraced: employers resist taking full responsibility, though some 20% *do* offer literacy education at work; at the same time, adult educators worry about employers' goals dominating at the expense of the learners, even as the educators increase their own status and expertise. Both employer and educators would seem to welcome the traditional division of labor, with the public sector supporting foundational learning, yet because the state lacks sufficient resources, private sector responsibility for literacy education is accepted and encouraged. Today, as in the early days of the republic, education advocates must play "the Franklin card," that is, subvert their liberal aims to those of funders that emphasize pragmatic education for work. Yet this seems a risky strategy, given all that is at stake in the current political environment. The concern is that if literacy is defined as solely for the purposes of employment, then other needs of the individual and the society may be overlooked, especially consequential for adult students, for whom this may be their only opportunity for formal education. Along slightly different lines, if literacy is defined primarily as a response to a competitiveness or school failure crisis, then, once the crisis is thought to abate, the support and funding for literacy may disappear as well. If the new schoolhouse is to fulfill its promise of educational opportunity, rather than be a place where workers "learn too much," this tension must be acknowledged and divergent views reconciled.

Shifting from ideology and policy, the focus will now turn to the real situations themselves—the literacy programs and the managers responsible for them. The first question to be addressed is why one-fifth of employers *do* offer basic skills education in the workplace. Managers' comments reveal that their motives are not simply educational, a finding that further illuminates the current construction of the literacy crisis and complicates the concern about employer control in the new schoolhouse.

NOTES

1. The test referred to was given as part of the National Adult Literacy Survey (NALS). Researchers sought to determine prose, document, and quantitative literacy using the types of materials and demands that the adults might encounter in their daily lives. This study differentiated five levels of literacy, a more complex assessment than the simplistic literate/illiterate assessments and the "grade level" determinations of the past, with greater diagnostic usefulness as well. Those adults at the lowest level, Level 1 (20-21%), could perform simple routine tasks involving brief and uncomplicated texts and documents—that is, even those at the lowest level could read, though competency ranged and was quite limited. One-fourth of those at this level were immigrants; another fourth had physical, mental, or health conditions that prohibited them from fully participating in work or school. Level 2, defined as able to locate information in a text, make low level inferences using printed materials, and integrate easily identifiable pieces of information, comprised 28%. These adults could also perform straightforward calculations. The next level encompassed nearly one-third of the survey participants. They could integrate information from relatively long or dense texts or documents, and could determine the appropriate arithmetic operation and identify quantities in a problem format. The final 18-21% performed at the highest two levels. The demographic breakdowns yielded no surprises—poor people performed at the lowest levels. See National Center for Educational Statistics, *National Adult Literacy Survey, Executive Summary* (Princeton, NJ: Educational Testing Service, 1993).

2. These data are from the "White Paper for 1999 National Literacy Forum," *NIFL Policy Update*, April 12, 1999.

3. National Literacy Act, Public Law 102-73, July 25, 1991.

4. For a useful early summation of the state of literacy services and the range of federal agencies involved, see Forrest P. Chisman, *Jump Start: The Federal Role in Adult Literacy* (Washington, DC: Southport Institute for Policy Analysis, 1989). Information about the ambivalence of the Department of Education with regard to funding workplace programs was gained from observations made during my tenure as a grants manager for

an economic development agency (1993-1994); subsequent review of policy documents corroborated these findings.

5. Kevin Hollenbeck's *Classrooms in the Workplace* (Kalamazoo, MI: W. E. Upjohn Institute for Employment Research, 1993) sets forth this breakdown, important since his focus is medium-sized and smaller businesses. Written by a labor economist, this book provides a useful description of efforts in one state, with findings (Chapter Two) that call into question the logic of human capital theory.

6. Both the adult literacy community and business community have publicly stated a desire for continued government support for workplace education (see the NIFL listserve archives and the Bloom and Lafleur 1999). That this has not occurred probably has more to do with politics than perceptions of efficacy. If the welfare reform bill is any indication, the sentiment of the Congress is that people belong in the workplace rather than in educational institutions, so it is surprising that there has been of yet no new allocation for workplace literacy. Family literacy is currently receiving the majority of federal funding set aside for special populations.

7. This quote is from an evaluation report prepared for the State of Massachusetts in 1991. It is not clear how widely the "new field" perception was shared, only that this group of consultants deemed it worthy of mentioning. See Laura Sperazi, Paul Jurmo, and David Rosen, "Participatory Approaches to Evaluating Outcomes and Designing Curriculum in Workplace Education Programs" (Newton, MA: Evaluation Research Inc., 1991): 3. Few of those who write about workplace literacy seem aware of the long history of workplace education, described later in this chapter.

8. These conclusions are from my interviews. Included in the sample were two highly unionized communications firms, as well as a state university. The respondent from the state had worked in union organizing for years, and offered a particularly useful perspective. These interview findings about the role of labor in encouraging workplace education are confirmed by other recent writings, for example, Katherine Dudley, *The End of the Line* (Chicago: University of Chicago, 1994).

9. Union activists advocate a broad type of education, called labor literacy, which includes adult basic education and ESL along with an emphasis on the creation of critical consciousness. Heavily influenced by participatory and radical philosophies, such labor education places the workers' interests as paramount, and takes it for granted that a fundamental realignment of power is needed in order to gain justice in the workplace. See Sheila Collins, "Workplace Literacy: Corporate Tool or Worker Empowerment?" *Social Policy* (Summer 1989): 26-30. An interview with a labor organizer involved in a long-standing literacy program at a public workplace affirmed this sentiment, and also suggested that unions had to go beyond literacy and challenge employers to "connect blue collar workers with career ladders."

10. New structures are emerging to make this possible. The successful Worker Centers in the garment industry are an example of an organizing tool that has education (particularly ESL) as a key mission, combined with consciousness. See Immanuel Ness, "Organizing Immigrant Communities: UNITE's Workers Center Strategy," in *Organizing to Win: New Research on Union Strategies,* edited by Kate Bronfenbrenner, et al. (Ithaca: ILR Press, 1998).

11. Considered one of the great thinkers on education, Paolo Freire has had his writings widely translated and applied. At the same time, these works have generated a significant stream of criticism. His seminal work is *Pedagogy of the Oppressed* (New York: Seabury, 1974), just reissued by Continuum Press. Subsequent writings have elaborated upon these themes and have taken on his critics, philosophical and methodological. See especially *Pedagogy of Hope* (New York: Continuum, 1992).

12. Citation from Henry A. Giroux, "What Is Literacy?" In *Becoming Political: Readings and Writings in the Politics of Literacy Education,* compiled by Patrick Shannon (Portsmouth, NH: Heinemann, 1992). One of the most prolific writers on the controversy surrounding literacy and work, as well as radical education reform, Giroux has written many articles and several books over the past decade. See *Teachers as Intellectuals: Toward a Critical Pedagogy of Learning* (Hadley, MA: Bergin and Garvey, 1988) and *Border Crossings: Cultural Workers and the Politics of Education* (New York: Routledge, 1992). Another influential work, with Stanley Aronowitz, is the critical analysis *Education Still Under Siege,* Second Edition (Westport, CT: Bergin & Garvey, 1993).

13. Occupations attain professional status through a predictable series of stages, as established by Harold Wilensky and other scholars of the professions. The classic article is Wilensky's "The Professionalization of Everyone?" *American Journal of Sociology* 2 (1964): 137-158. One motivation for undertaking a professionalization project is power—elite professionals wield a great deal of material and cultural clout in our society, and have traditionally played a social trusteeship role as well. (See Brint, cited below, for discussion.)

14. Professionalization as a source of organizational change is detailed by Paul J. DiMaggio and Walter W. Powell in "The Iron Cage Revisited: Institutional Isomorphism and Collective Rationality in Organizational Fields," *American Sociological Review* (April 1983): 147-160. They assert that the normative pressure exerted by professionals serves to make organizations similar to each other, alongside pressures from the state and from other firms.

15. Findings in this section are drawn primarily from my grant management experience writing and reviewing program proposals. Part of my planning responsibilities involved assuring that funds were spent as budget guidelines required. Documentation can be found in the annual state plans filed with the Department of Labor, as well as in the Federal Register where new funding streams are announced.

16. The diminishment of the social responsibility of the professional strata is the thesis of Steven Brint, *In an Age of Experts: The Changing Role of Professionals in Politics and Public Life* (Princeton, NJ: Princeton University Press, 1994). Brint also discusses the conservative politics of many in the human services (59). For critical perspective that focuses on the rising power of firms and managers versus professionals, see Charles Derber, William Schwartz, and Yale Magrass, *Power in the Highest Degree: Professionals and the Rise of the New Mandarin Order* (New York: Oxford University Press, 1990).

17. The organizational employment of professionals is a controversial and extensively analyzed subject because of the theoretical dichotomy between organizational loyalty and professional allegiance. Richard Hall's 1968 article set forth the groundwork for the topic, "Professionalization and Bureaucratization," *American Sociological Review* 33: 92-104. Magali Larson developed the idea from a critical (and international) perspective in *The Rise of Professionalism: A Sociological Analysis* (Berkeley: University of California Press, 1977). What is less commonly noted is the way in which the tension surrounding organizational employment can assist the professionalization process in newly emerging specialties.

18. Andrew Abbott refers to this as the process of establishing "jurisdictional control," important as interprofessional battles are joined. Adult educators appear to win this battle in the workplace, by carving out jurisdiction over basic skills and literacy education. See *The System of Professions: An Essay on the Division of Expert Labor* (Chicago: University of Chicago Press, 1988).

19. Kett, in *The Pursuit of Knowledge Under Difficulties* (1994), suggests that these contradictions are not new. He warns, "Exploring the history of continuing and adult education entails making sense of astounding statistics, frustratingly loose terminology, lofty idealism and base hucksterism" (xi).

20. See the International Literacy Explorer web site published by University of Pennsylvania Graduate School of Education for comparative statistics based on UNESCO data: <http://www.literacyonline.org/explorer/stats_basic.html>

21. Jerome Bruner made this argument most persuasively in his "Introduction" to *Literacy: An Overview by Fourteen Experts,* edited by Stephen R. Graubaud (New York: Hill and Wang, 1991).

22. For a nuanced explanation of this phenomenon, see Carl E. Kaestle et al., *Literacy in the United States: Readers and Reading since 1880* (New Haven: Yale University Press, 1991). These authors, like many others, acknowledge that "complete" illiteracy must be considered differently than functional literacy, the type of literacy that is context dependent. The NALS test, a description of which began the chapter, is considered a test of functional literacy.

23. This theme was developed by Henry Resnik, writing in Graubaud's volume *Literacy: An Overview by Fourteen Experts*, 170. Paolo Friere is the source of ideas about literacy and power, described in a less polemical fashion by several of the "fourteen experts."

24. For multiple perspectives on this see the Shannon compilation *Becoming Political* (1992). This book is especially useful because of the range of educational sites and literacy levels addressed.

25. This assessment is according to John Trimbur, cited in a column by Jim Dempsey, "Current Literacy Crisis Is Just the Latest," *Worcester Telegram and Gazette* (February 17, 1992). Trimbur's writing is also found in the book *Becoming Political,* compiled by Shannon (1992).

26. Quote is from Trimbur (1992). Sheryl Gowen explores the current public discourse of a workplace literacy crises in *The Politics of Workplace Literacy* (New York: Teachers College Press, 1992), 13-15. She writes, "When major social change occurs, the *perception* of a literacy crisis is often one of the first indicators" (13).

27. Dunlop's query was about the proper role of the private versus the public sector in provision of such human services, but his apprehension went largely unheeded. The Dunlop quote is from a book by Ernest A. Lynton, *The Missing Connection Between Business and the Universities* (New York: American Council on Education/Macmillan, 1984). The shadow metaphor was further developed by Robert L. Craig and Christine J. Evers, "Employers and Educators: The Shadow Education System," in *Business and Higher Education: Toward a New Alliance,* edited by Gerard G. Gold (San Francisco: Jossey-Bass, 1981).

28. See U.S. Congress, Office of Technology Assessment, *Worker Training: Competing in the New Economy,* OTA-ITE-457 (Washington, DC: U.S. Government Printing Office, 1990).

29. I make this argument in "Immigrant Workers and the Shadow Education System," *Education Policy* 13 (1999): 251-279.

3

Justifying the Education Strategy: Learning and Legitimacy

Literacy has a direct impact on economic prosperity, for individuals and their work organizations. Yet according to the 1999 International Adult Literacy Survey, more than 40% of the U.S. workforce did not have the basic skills needed to do their job, and only a fraction of these workers were enrolled in educational programs. Whether this is a crisis manufactured to serve a larger social need, or whether this is the root of productivity problems is to a certain extent irrelevant. What matters is that employers, educators, policy makers and union leaders perceive the literacy problem in the workplace as real. What these groups cannot agree upon is who is responsible for resolution. The boundary blurring in the contemporary political environment complicates the issue: while no one suggests fully privatizing the adult education system, the idea of employer sponsorship has its supporters.

Despite efforts of the public sector to encourage privately (or jointly) funded workplace literacy programs, the majority of employers do not think that rectifying the literacy problem is their responsibility. A 1995 Opinion Research Corporation survey states, "Although 90 percent of Fortune 1000 CEOs recognize illiteracy as a tragedy in the U.S.workplace, many executives are reluctant to admit that some of their workers may be illiterate and do not necessarily feel that it is their problem to fix" (Reese 1996:14-15). In keeping with the traditional division of institutional labor, most employers believe that the illiteracy "tragedy" should be a public sector responsibility, notwithstanding the direct impact on their businesses. The fact that only a minority of companies chooses an education strategy despite facing similar external labor and competitive market conditions indicates that this is a meaningful decision, if not a bold one, on the part of the managers involved.[1] What accounts for such a decision? This chapter will present managers' own explanations for the implementation and persistence of workplace literacy programs, and will begin to analyze the inconsistencies in their justifications. I will then explore the extent to which the education strategy may reflect a desire for organizational legitimacy as much as an attempt to provide skills and knowledge.

WHY THE NEW SCHOOLHOUSE? MANAGERS' INTERPRETATIONS

Managers that select the education strategy obviously have other choices, since workplace education is not a widespread solution, nor is it predictable for a given industry or production technology.[2] Consequently, managerial discretion is high. Managers were enthusiastic about discussing their reasons for sponsoring literacy education in the workplace, and had strong opinions about these programs.[3] I sought to understand their justifications by direct questioning and by indirectly addressing the issue. First, they were explicitly asked to name their two main motives for implementing such programs. These motives have been tabulated and clustered into three categories: employee expertise, competitive pressures, and employee well-being.

TABLE 1

COMPANY MOTIVES FOR SPONSORING LITERACY

EMPLOYEE EXPERTISE	
Skills	9
Communication	9
Technology	5
COMPETITIVE PRESSURES	
Customer	5
Retention	5
Safety	4
Quality	4
Regulation	2
Union	2
EMPLOYEE WELL-BEING	
Participation	2
Self-development	2
Benefit	1

Overall, these responses echo taken-for-granted beliefs about why employers would invest in literacy education for their employees. Even so, the three categories reveal several contradictions. The *employee expertise* category encompasses the most frequent responses and reflects customary reasons for any type of education—the improvement of skills and communication abilities, with the goal being knowledge and language proficiency. Technology is included in this category because managers mentioned that basic literacy was needed so those employees could be prepared for new software or hardware. Skills, communication, and technology can be considered instrumental motives for implementing a literacy program, consistent with the rationale of business groups and policy advocates. Other researchers have come to similar conclusions with regard to the typical reasons that employers cite.[4]

The next set of responses—customer service, employee retention, safety requirements, quality pressures, regulatory changes, and union negotiation—are prevalent concerns in contemporary work organizations as *competitive pressures* mount. What is interesting is that they are being tackled through the provision of literacy education, education being only one of the strategies that a company might select in the face of these external pressures. To illustrate the alternatives: companies may choose to enhance customer service by hiring college graduates, or may improve quality through a reward system or process innovation. Therefore, when managers report that they select the education strategy for a reason in the competitive category, I suggest that their motives are noneducative. Given what has been said about the ideological power of education in American culture, the presumption is made that the literacy programs have symbolic meanings, since education is being used to address organizational issues other than expertise.

The final three items: participation, self-development, and benefits, are not customary reasons for corporate education either, though this *employee well-being* category contains responses that educators might offer when asked about the purpose of education. That some managers acknowledge such motives is noteworthy, and may suggest that a sense of enlightened self-interest or altruism accompanies (or displaces) bottom line decisions with regard to literacy education. An alternative interpretation is that employee well-being leads indirectly to productive and loyal employees. Yet this begs the question: if well being is sought, why *education*? Other types of benefits (particularly financial) might offer the same result, with greater opportunity for corporate control over the outcome. Again, education apparently carries symbolic value, and the education strategy has utility beyond the provision of simple literacy.

Thus, managers' explicit justifications are largely congruent with corporate and government policy statements regarding the provision of employer-sponsored education: companies provide literacy education to enhance employee expertise, which in turn allows them to respond to competitiveness pressures.[5] The key finding is that the majority of the motives mentioned could be addressed by means other than education, leading to the conclusion that the literacy programs have symbolic value to the organizations and the managers themselves. The nature of the symbolism attached to literacy education becomes visible as managers consider other issues related to literacy education. Underlying the espoused desire for employee expertise is the wish to exhibit humanitarian values as well as a desire to retain existing employees.

Values and Retention

Given that only about one fifth of workplaces are thought to offer literacy education, despite apparent widespread need, it is obvious that most employers do *not* choose an education policy in order to address competitiveness issues. Alternatives in the current competitive environment are ample: downsizing, outsourcing, diversification, and merging, among others. Even companies that acknowledge a "skill gap" do not necessarily respond with an investment in education. Their options include deskilling jobs, investing in technology rather than people, or replacing existing employees with already literate workers. Managers were asked why they chose education rather than laying off current workers and hiring more literate workers, or redesigning jobs, or moving offshore. Their answers were value-laden and deeply felt, and benefit from quotation rather than quantification. It is noteworthy that the logic of the marketplace is not the predominant theme when managers explain their reasons for investing in existing employees. One said simply:

> I think companies owe it to employees.
> *Training and Development Manager,*
> *Large Bank*

Several others spoke explicitly of commitment and loyalty, along with retention:

> The hospital has a commitment to retention and development. Basic jobs need to be done. [This] shows the hospital's commitment and caring, which is important.
> *Training Director,*
> *Regional Hospital*

> We have a commitment to our current employees. This is a wonderful, wonderful staff that happens not to speak English. We want all our employees to better themselves.
> *Director of Inservice,*
> *Long Term Care Facility*

> We have long-time, loyal good workers and hate to lose those kinds of people. We give them every opportunity to grow.
> *Human Resources Manager,*
> *Small Community Hospital*

Commitment and loyalty were not mentioned when managers were asked directly why they sponsored literacy education, yet these issues are highlighted when the logic of educating current workers is questioned. This finding illuminates the nature of the symbolic meaning proffered by literacy programs: such programs signal that these companies value existing employees. This was a message that the managers were happy to repeat and with which they clearly identified. They believed that "education is good," returning to the quotes that opened Chapter One, and also wanted to believe that their companies were good, because they offered education and because they were committed to existing employees. So employer-sponsored literacy education can be thought of as symbolizing the humane (or ethical) aspects of corporate culture. Additional comments bear out this supposition. One person, from a company internationally renowned for its strong moral values, stated bluntly,

> In the short term that may perhaps be advantageous from a business point of view, but we think that would be very close to unethical and I think long term we'd be shooting ourselves in the foot, anyway. They got us to where we are today.
>
> *Human Resources Director,*
> *Global Health Product Manufacturer*

Another respondent called upon personal rather than organizational ethics, saying,

> I wouldn't work in a place that treated people like that.
>
> *Workplace Education Director,*
> *Small Telecommunications Factory*

So in choosing the education strategy, rather than other options, these companies are interested in more than increasing employee expertise. They want to increase the expertise of *existing* employees, implying that retention is a key value (as mentioned by five of those surveyed). Yet managers do not admit that these low-level employees are retained because they are low-cost. In the managerial rhetoric, employees are not "treated like that" because the employer is ethical and humane. Retention is framed in terms of loyalty, rather than cost-effectiveness.

Another set of responses builds upon these values, as managers differentiate their organization from other firms that are presumably less humane. Several health care managers interpreted employer-sponsored education as evidence of their caring culture, and one person explicitly differentiated himself from the business sector, saying derisively (and inaccurately),[6]

> People in health care will take a risk. [You] wouldn't get a plant manager to put people in an ESL class.
>
> *Human Resources Manager,*
> *Small Community Hospital*

However, plant managers *do* put people in literacy classes, of all types. And they espouse values of care and retention. Several manufacturing managers' rationales are stated below, in response to the question about why they would offer education rather than replace existing workers with literate workers:

We don't do that—we really care.
Workplace Education Director,
Small Telecommunication Factory

We don't lay off.

Education Specialist,
Electronics Firm

We want loyalty and longevity.

Training Manager,
Global Hardware Manufacturer

Their use of the first person plural, "we," serves to distinguish the respondent's own organization from organizations in general, organizations that by implication are less worthwhile. These managers identify with their employers' values, and want these values to be distinctive. Although differentiation does not appear on a list of reasons for selecting the education strategy, it can be understood as another symbolic motive. The value of differentiation is that it enhances the managers' beliefs that their organizations are humane and ethical, and keeps them from looking carefully at the basis of those beliefs. Differentiation is made manifest through education and retention of employees, explicitly those at the bottom of the hierarchy.

Not all managers responded in ways that can be interpreted as value-laden: a few disagreed that the labor market was strong enough to supply literate job applicants, or that literacy levels were determinable prior to employment. Several others were prohibited from layoffs by union contracts, and these firms chose an education strategy because of bargaining terms. Employer-sponsored education may be a less meaningful choice in these firms, though it still allows retention of inexpensive, low-level employees.

Considering these qualitative comments about loyalty, caring, and ethics in the context of the responses tabulated earlier, a more nuanced picture emerges as to why employers sponsor literacy education. Educative reasons are initially espoused, though symbolic motivations are not far below the surface. When probed, corporate and personal values emerge. That managers do not describe education in economically calculable terms is significant—instead, they use the language of betterment, fairness, and commitment. To these managers, workplace literacy programs are symbolic of an ethical and humane organization, a type of organization that they believe is not found everywhere. Based on these data, the question "Why workplace literacy?" might be answered, "Because it symbolizes our reliance upon existing employees and our desire to keep them with our organization, and therefore that this is a worthy and unusual place to work," rather than, "Because we need employees with a certain set of skills." Perhaps both answers are true to a certain extent; on the other hand, the combination of these answers may obscure explanations that are less appealing to the middle managers interviewed.

Managers may be reluctant to resort to the external labor market for several reasons: perhaps they cannot pay the wages that truly literate employees may demand, or maybe the jobs are not appealing to those with higher skills. It is also possible that attitude is more important than skills. Alternatively, like other "make or buy" decisions that a manager must make, the decision to educate current employees may allow the employer greater influence over the outcome. Yet these managers do not say, "We need low-cost loyal compliant workers who haven't been taught too much." Instead, they rely upon the education ideology, with its promise of opportunity and aura of fairness. (There is evidence that cost, control, and attitude are unanticipated consequences of the new schoolhouse, which will be addressed in later chapters.)

To summarize, firms select the education strategy for noneducative reasons, not all that surprising given the role played by education in the broader society. The education strategy allows organizations to perpetuate humane and ethical values, and to differentiate themselves from competitors. Within the workplace, the education strategy is seen as an expression of organizational values more so than an economically desirable or calculable solution. An organizational culture that purports to value people may be appealing to employees, and appears to engender pride on the part of the managers. Education symbolizes organizational commitment and loyalty, and education engenders organizational commitment, by demonstrating a humane and ostensibly unique corporate culture. These organizational values are further revealed in managers' comments concerning employer responsibility for education.

BELIEFS ABOUT EMPLOYER RESPONSIBILITY

In addition to specific questions about why their companies sponsored literacy education, managers were asked what they thought about the private sector in general becoming more responsible for education, in short, becoming the new schoolhouse. Their responses elucidate the complex and contradictory meanings attached to the decision to sponsor literacy education in the workplace, and the subsequent blurring of the private/public boundaries. Four divergent perspectives on the educator role can be identified: paternalistic, fatalistic, collaborative, and conditional.

Several managers used language of fairness, justice, and beneficence to propose that employers *should* be responsible for basic education. These quotes illustrate an awareness of the fundamental power imbalances between firm and worker, and echo paternalistic rationalizations for firm behavior:

> The employer's responsibility is to create an environment [for learning], because they have the most power.
>
> *Director of Training,*
> *Small Hospital*

> Some people don't get the right cards dealt. The company's responsibility is to offer another card.
>
> *Manager of Human Resources,*
> *Medium-sized Distribution Center*

> Employer's responsibility to employees should include education for better service and better quality of life. There are broad areas of mutual benefit if this happens.
>
> *Human Resources Manager,*
> *Nursing Home*

Yet this was a limited sense of responsibility, and did not extend beyond the organization. When probed as to whether they acted out of a sense of social responsibility, it became apparent that their focus was internal. As one stated,

> Social responsibility didn't enter our thinking. We were concerned about our employees—the microcosm of society here.
>
> *Administrator,*
> *Long Term Care Facility*

Again, the theme seems to be treating the current labor force well, affirming the image of the firm as humane and value-driven, and aspiring to "broad areas of mutual benefit." This echoes the paternalistic attitudes of employers, believed to be obsolete. Rather than rectify the power imbalance, firms that operate with this philosophy are at the same time benevolent and oppressive.

In contrast, a group of managers thought about their responsibility for literacy in an instrumental and nearly fatalistic vein, using the rationale that the firm "had no choice." Several reiterated the rationale of the policy makers as to the skill gap and the failure of the schools:

> A lot of people come in and we end up training them on things you assume that coming out of college, they would know. We take up the slack.
>
> *Education Specialist,*
> *Manufacturing Firm*

> We have no choice. Key reason is what you read—high schools are not preparing students adequately.
>
> *Training Manager,*
> *Multi-national High Tech Firm*

Also speaking from a fatalistic perspective were those who mentioned the convenience associated with workplace programs, and the perpetual nature of technological change.

There is no time otherwise—most have two jobs and family responsibilities. The only place that's available for learning is the workplace.

Employment Specialist,
Large Teaching Hospital

In general we have no choice. With so much change, it is a necessity to be learning. This has been recognized in medicine forever.

Human Resource Director,
Medium-sized Hospital

Crucial to the fatalistic rationale is the belief that *employers* were responsible for "taking up the slack." This could become a significant responsibility for employers, though, and one manager said his firm was taking on the schoolhouse role only for the short term.

Until more opportunities become available, private industry must pick up the slack.

Human Resources Director,
Large Manufacturer

From this perspective, employers take responsibility reluctantly, and temporarily. The "no choice" answers are interesting but not persuasive, since other opportunities *are* available, and many companies make the choice of a strategy other than education. Perhaps the managers must convince themselves that they have no choice because the new schoolhouse is such a challenge to accepted notions of employer scope. Or managers may have internalized societal messages about the necessity for redrawing the boundaries between public and private responsibility. It is also possible that managers have adopted the education solution rather unthinkingly, unable to see other options because of its ideological power and proffered legitimacy. Whatever the explanation, the fatalism of the "no choice" rationale is a significant finding, as is the idea of shared responsibility.

In the third view, the private sector, the public sector, and the individual in need of literacy education share responsibility. Managers who espouse this view do not expect the public sector to own the problem or the solution, as do the "no choice" believers, nor do they think employers alone should be responsible as do those labeled paternalistic. Rather, managers expect employees, schools, and firms to work together. Several stated this explicitly when asked about the extent of employer responsibility:

A joint effort. Home is important too. A lot of people graduate but their skills need work. Schools should do more.

Training Director,
Financial Services Firm

> I am charging the corporation with the responsibility to take responsibility. They shouldn't be the sole providers of education, but they should certainly have a big hand in it.
>
> *Program Administrator,*
> *Multi-state Bank*

The expectation that adult literacy be a collaborative effort is significant because of the bridge this creates between the public and private sectors. Rather than blur boundaries, collaboration rises above them. The fact that the individual workers are expected to be responsible is important as well, since it indicates a marked change from the paternalistic notions of the past, a change particularly significant when the subject is education. The expectation of increased individual responsibility, evident in other aspects of the new workplace, can also be interpreted negatively, as further "blaming the victim." This individualization of the employment relationship is a theme that reverberates throughout the new schoolhouse analysis and will be considered at length in a subsequent chapter.

Not all managers agreed that firms should shoulder any type of responsibility for general education, even though they worked in firms already offering literacy education programs. Again, reasons diverged, based on the extent to which the curriculum was work-related. One conditional perspective is made evident in the following quote:

> There are limits to the employers' responsibility. From the hospital's point of view, if it is not job related we don't see it [education] as a big commitment.
>
> *Human Resources Director,*
> *Large Teaching Hospital*

This manager articulates the rationale of human capital theory: employers should support job-related education because there is direct benefit to the organization. The next manager quoted has an entirely different reason for being concerned about corporate responsibility for education. She is worried that broader goals will be lost if firms take control:

> From where I am coming from philosophically, I get nervous when we start talking about corporations providing education because I know they are going to do it to their advantage. And I am a classicist when it comes to education—I think that people should have the ability to study Keats and Yeats and stuff like that so I worry a little bit about the corporations tailoring, of course Business Writing, Business Math, and the creativeness is something else again. I support the government (as education provider)—because I know, being inside this indus-

> try that if the government wasn't there saying that you have to reinvest, then you don't believe for a minute that we would be.
>
> *Senior Program Administrator,*
> *Multi-State Bank*

Like several other managers with whom I spoke, this person distanced her own values ("where I am coming from philosophically") from those of her employer, and worried about the noneducational motives of the corporation. Such individuals are skeptical about the boundary blurring made evident by the new schoolhouse, and prefer the checks and balances of the traditional division of institutional responsibility.

Although there is not a universally embraced sense of responsibility among these managers, their comments reveal acceptance of a more extensive role for employers with regard to general education. This role can take several forms: paternalistic, fatalistic, collaborative, and conditional. Nearly all revealed a degree of reluctance, either economic or philosophical. Not surprisingly, the reluctance was derived from the organizations' primary role as a work organization, not a schoolhouse. Corporate managers tend to be more pragmatic than philosophical, yet even in their pragmatism they address the issue of blurred boundaries.[7] While these managers are aware of the tension between business and educational goals, their concerns are more mundane—they are interested in productive employees, and they are dependent on their current labor force. Workers are *not* entirely disposable in the new economy, despite layoffs and downsizing. At the same time, they are aware of the blurring of boundaries, and uneasy with the changing role of the firm. The question of employer responsibility is unsettled, with a range of perspectives offered by those inside the firm. From the outside the organization as well, the question of responsibility has multiple interpretations.

WHY THE NEW SCHOOLHOUSE? PRESSURES FOR LEGITIMACY

Social Responsibility

When I told acquaintances that I was doing research on workplace literacy programs, they remarked along the lines of either, "Isn't it nice that companies do that?" or "Do they do it just for public relations?" These beliefs in corporate largesse or cynicism about apparent largesse provide further evidence that literacy programs have meaning beyond simple education. Whether middle managers acknowledge it or not, companies may sponsor workplace literacy programs because of their philosophy of social responsibility, or, less altruistically, because of a desire to gain a better reputation. Senior executives may believe that literacy education offers legitimacy to their strategic actions.[8]

Attention to social responsibility and reputation have increased in recent years, and both have been correlated positively with bottom line results, allowing companies to argue that they can "do well" while "doing good."[9] Workplace literacy programs epitomize such practices. The Boston Chamber of Commerce named two of the firms I studied "exemplary" in a public and publicized award ceremony, a designation that added to their positive reputation in the community. Moreover, companies that offer literacy education may do so because they define themselves as socially responsible, notwithstanding middle managers' comments to the contrary. One study determined that the provision of basic skills training is more likely in firms whose CEOs articulate proactive corporate social responsibility philosophies (Anderson 1993). This researcher concluded that social responsibility philosophies were independent of organizational variables, having found little evidence that either skill shortages or union pressures resulted in employer-sponsored education and training. These findings strengthen the conclusion that basic skills training is not necessarily offered for educational reasons, such as need for skilled workers, but rather for symbolic reasons.

Symbolic actions by firms can be perceived negatively, but cynicism about the superficiality of reputation as a motive is countered by the reality that tangible accomplishments are the source of the approbation. In other words, even if the motivation is "only PR," the activity is significant. Again, firms can "get good PR" by any number of means, so the question remains, why *education*? Because the rational explanations are plausible but incomplete, alternative explanations must be determined. The institutional perspective on organizational behavior offers one set of alternatives, and is particularly useful because it takes legitimacy as a central concept. This approach to understanding "why education?" focuses on pressures that are not necessarily explicitly acknowledged by the managers involved.

Education and Legitimacy

As now should be recognized, corporations use education for symbolic as well as educative purposes, in keeping with the popularity of the education solution in American culture. Managers are influenced by these cultural norms, as well as by their beliefs about what is valued in their workplace. At the same time, beliefs about the public/private division of responsibility for education allow managers to articulate their varied understandings of the new schoolhouse. In addition to all the explanations that managers identified above, there are external pressures that may influence a manager considering literacy programs. Often, though not always, the manager is unaware of the ways in which these pressures affect them. These factors include cultural beliefs, state regulations, industry expectations, and the pressures brought to bear on workplaces by other constituents: learners themselves, and adult educators.[10] Appearing to respond to these influences can result in legitimacy for the organization and its members, according to institutional theory. And legitimacy is thought to be as crucial to organizational survival as organizational efficiency.[11]

Rational Myths: Ideology, Uncertainty, Demographics, and Politics

The education ideology is the first factor examined as possible institutional explanations for the new schoolhouse are considered. To reiterate, beliefs about individual freedom, equality for all, and the role of education in a democracy are tied to rhetoric concerning competitiveness, future work skills, and literacy. In this belief system, education is the solution to social and economic problems, and is blamed when problems persist. In institutional parlance, these are "rational myths" that reflect widely shared social rules and belief systems.[12] Rational myths are evident at a nonspecific cultural level, yet can also wield influence through less amorphous aspects of the environment: the traditional education system, the economy, demographics, and politics.

The well-established and highly legitimate system of K-16 education is the strongest institutional influence on companies that select the educational strategy. Because of shared, if inchoate, ideological expectations, work organizations have increased their expenditures on education and training, often without careful analysis of costs and benefits, or attention to outcomes. Data from manager interviews, as well as findings of other researchers, back up this assertion. Managers believe that "education is a good thing," to return to the quote that opened Chapter One. Moreover, instruction is on the rise in nearly all societies, and therefore the increase in employer-sponsored training can be understood as reflecting this global trend.[13] Such cultural pressures may not be strong enough to assure that a majority of employers offer literacy education, but the value accorded to education provides community approbation and straightforward justification for those that do select this strategy. They do not have to explain much when asked, "why education?" Its value is taken for granted. The education ideology exerts mimetic pressure: the traditional system influences the shadow system to become more "school-like," with formalized learning, designated educators, and credentials.

Second, institutional analysis calls our attention to one particularly influential aspect of the economy, that of uncertainty (Oliver 1991). The thesis is that organizations operating in environments with high uncertainty will attempt to establish the illusion or reality of control and stability over future organizational outcomes; they also will be more likely to imitate other organizations. Employers have a bias towards action in the face of uncertainty, and education is a relatively inexpensive and universally valued action that on the surface seems a logical response to economic uncertainty. This solution, education, is vague enough to address what cannot be known (particularly if carried out in the spirit of Socrates, rather than the pragmatists). A narrow choice, for example to train workers in a new technology or hire employees with a specific skill, is only a short term solution, certainly valued by many but difficult to justify given the seemingly perpetual nature of economic uncertainty. As one hospital manager stated, "With so much change, it is a necessity to be learning." While the constant change may be more evident inside of work organizations, external economic pressures get the attention of managers, particularly those at the senior levels. Employer-sponsored literacy education can be explained as an attempt to minimize environmental uncertainty by signaling that the firm is acting positively, by improving the abilities and knowledge of the workforce. Whether or not literacy education actually results in more flexible organizations is not the point. Such efforts symbolize that the company intends to respond proactively to external pressures, and proactive response will engender legitimacy.

Beliefs about demographic changes, however myth-like, also partially explain the decision of an employer to invest in workforce education. Three managers, without prompting, cited the Department of Labor funded report *Workforce 2000* (Johnston and Packer 1987) as having influenced their decision to offer literacy education, and as being the key argument used to persuade senior management of the need for such programs. *Workforce 2000* asserted that from 1985 to 2000 the U.S. workforce would grow slowly, becoming older, more female, and more disadvantaged, and that the new jobs in service industries will demand much higher skill levels than the jobs of today. To address these concerns, the authors suggested that black and Hispanic workers be integrated more fully into the economy and that the educational preparation of all workers be improved. *Workforce 2000* was referenced in the national media, government policy statements, and on university reading lists—a significant accomplishment for a government report. The overall findings were interpreted to mean that companies had to provide basic skills themselves if they wanted to plan for the future. The managers who alluded to the report did not question this belief.

Yet deeper scrutiny reveals irrationality and suggests institutional forces at work. Above all, *Workforce 2000* is limited as a planning document because the data it set forth were national in scale, not all that useful to managers working in specific, local labor markets. Though state policy documents urged that local demographic conditions be taken into account, the managers interviewed for this study did not articulate their concerns in local terms. Managers asserted, as *Workforce 2000* predicted, that their future labor force entrants would not be able to speak English or do algebra well enough to do the kind of jobs that would need doing. That they did not question *Workforce 2000* shows the embeddedness of beliefs about the inadequate skills of the workforce, and provides evidence of the "bandwagon" effect that institutional theory tries to explain. *Workforce 2000* was eventually discredited in the academic press because of faulty population numbers and inaccurate presumptions about educational levels,[14] yet managers' beliefs (and perhaps fears) were such that the quality of the data were not questioned.

A fourth rational myth that influences employers considering the sponsorship of literacy education concerns the private/public collaborations believed to expedite such efforts. As one manager asserted, "Together we stand, divided we fall." Employers reported being urged to work with state educational agencies and community colleges, even if their companies were not seeking public funding. Collaboration was fundamental to the program models supported by the National Workplace Literacy Initiative—the educational provider agreed to work with employers and the union to determine students' needs, and then to jointly determine the optimal time for classes, etc. The myth-like nature of the

collaborative rhetoric is revealed by the fact that it appears to be primarily symbolic. In reality, power to make decisions about employer-sponsored literacy
education resides in the private sector, a concern to those who see the public
sector and/or organized labor as providing a necessary counterweight to the influence of the market. Nonetheless, an emphasis on collaboration appears to be
one consequence of the boundary blurring in the political environment, and may
be taken for granted by managers who have increased their outsourcing and entered joint ventures of all sorts. Collaborative pressures appear to minimize the
distinction between the organization and its external environment, allowing the
new schoolhouse to be an acceptable innovation, albeit justified by reasons that
are not necessarily educational.

The rational myths influencing workplace literacy are several: the
power of the education solution, its ability to temper economic uncertainty, the
prospect of an uneducated labor force, and the egalitarian solution of collaboration. By responding to these macro level pressures through the sponsorship of
literacy education, employers achieve a type of moral legitimacy, based on
structures and procedures. Managers reflect this moral legitimacy through their
pride in their literacy programs, and their assertion that the activity is the "right
thing to do."[15] Moral legitimacy can be contrasted with the pragmatic legitimacy
brought about by pressures closer to the work organization, from the state and
industry sectors.

"Red Tape" and Industry Pressures

Despite the expectations of private sector dominance in the contemporary political environment, public sector pressures on firms that sponsor employer-sponsored literacy education are palpable, particularly so in Massachusetts during the early 1990s. The state offered direct funding and indirect monetary incentives to start-up workplace literacy programs, with the expectation that
employers would eventually take on full responsibility. Tax credits were also
available to offset educational expenses, a traditional mechanism for encouraging private support. Less traditional incentives to take responsibility were also
evident. For example, in Massachusetts, community colleges were required to
find external revenue streams, and one such stream was workplace training and
basic skills education, funded by the employers. Several managers said that they
would not have offered literacy education onsite without community college
encouragement and services, evidence for the influence of the state.

State agencies also have the power to direct the shape of the workplace
programs, as outlined in the previous discussion of collaboration. Companies
that receive public grants are given a set of guidelines with regard to teacher
selection, class structure, curriculum, and so forth. Yet, as is inherent in the
rhetoric of collaboration, the state cannot dictate these decisions. Rather, state
funders make recommendations and suggest which parties should be consulted.
Nonetheless, if future grant money is desired, it is in the firm's best interests to
follow these guidelines, as well as to comply with state reporting requirements.

The state's presence is occasionally perceived as overly coercive. Several interviewees reported that their companies refused state funding. The reasons cited were paperwork and programmatic requirements, that is, the red tape that went along with the grant. That these companies were willing to support literacy education themselves shows acceptance of the schoolhouse role, though again, this acceptance may be more pragmatic than philosophical. Only half the firms in my sample received any state funding, further indication of the limits of state influence on companies that are interested in the topic of workforce literacy. Obviously, pressure from the state is relatively minimal when considered from a broader perspective. The state does not sanction employers without literacy programs, nor does it regulate existing programs beyond assuring that guidelines are adhered to for continued funding.

Despite these frictions, the state pressures result in a simple pragmatic legitimacy, which may be useful to managers as they attempt to justify their investments or assure that their programs continue. Yet this is hardly enough, especially since the legitimacy offered by government involvement has diminished as public sector has power lessened. Companies must seek alternative sources of legitimacy, provided by their industries in conjunction with the state.

Beyond Red Tape: Tensions in Health Care and Banking[16]

Two industry-specific legal requirements in particular were commented upon by the respondents: the Community Reinvestment Act (CRA), the federal banking legislation that mandates deposits be used to benefit the neighboring citizens; and the Joint Commission of Accreditation of Hospitals (JCAH) standards with which hospitals are expected to comply. Three bank managers (of four in the sample) mentioned the Community Reinvestment Act as part of the reason they offered workplace literacy education, their rationale being that the educational programs help less fortunate individuals and therefore fulfill the goal of community investment. CRA compliance, real and "paper," has been a public topic nationwide due to the number of banks that have sought approval for large mergers, and the subsequent vocal response from activists, particularly in Massachusetts. As a result, senior bank management is highly aware of the CRA, and no doubt this worry has filtered down through the ranks to the middle managers such as those in this study. Still, activities such as educational programs for workers were not the intent of the original law, since the legislation was designed to counteract redlining practices and to help neighborhood residents and businesses gain access to capital. None of the banks reported opening their literacy classes to local people or employees' families, in contrast to several hospitals that did so. Yet managers used this broadly worded regulation to support literacy education for bank workers.

Broad interpretation is also the case in the health care industry. In this era of health care reform, hospital closings, and managed care, accreditation is ever more important for hospitals, so the pressure that the JCAH wields is broad and deep, though often nonspecific. JCAH regulations have been loosely interpreted to justify investment in literacy improvements, though the regulations do not mandate either literacy or education. One manager was careful to explain:

> JCAH wants "competent workforce at all levels" not just patient care—this is new. Their issue is customer satisfaction—this is not a standard regarding literacy or language ability, per se. Health care has become more competitive. Patients are more educated and have higher expectations. Communication has become very important. Patients expect that everyone wearing a hospital uniform can communicate and help them.
>
> *Human Resource Director,*
> *Medium-sized Hospital*

The overall issue is customer satisfaction, with communication ability the core expectation. That this is addressed through educational programs is not as surprising in the health care industry as it might be in other industries, for several reasons. One has to do with the history of hospitals as teaching environments, and the second with the institutional culture of caring. These institutional characteristics are perhaps even more consequential than the JCAH influence.

While a full analysis of the industry-specific pressures is beyond the scope of this book, several telling anecdotes suggest that a cursory review of the tensions in health care and financial services may further explain the institutionalization of workplace literacy programs. Hospital administrators commented upon the uniqueness of the health care field with respect to worker education; and one banker had a surprising response to the literacy issue as a whole.

In the first section of this chapter, I quoted a hospital manager who asserted that, "People in health care will take a risk. [You] wouldn't get a plant manager to put people in an ESL class." While this was an inaccurate statement, it revealed much about the perceived uniqueness of the norms and values in the health care field. These norms are important to understanding why the health service firms offer literacy programs, especially in the current political environment. The fact that these norms are being challenged as market mechanisms are brought to bear in this industry makes it likely that managers will hold to them all the more energetically. The teaching hospitals are the high status health care providers, and exert a disproportionate influence. They consider themselves to be as much educational institutions as health care providers. In such workplaces, ongoing education is taken for granted for all professionals, from lab technician to medical doctor, so it is not difficult to justify such investments for lower level workers, especially since everyone is expected to become more involved in patient care. Onsite classes are a regular occurrence in hospitals, and the twenty-four hour shift builds in flexibility and diminishes the scheduling and coverage issues encountered in more traditional workplaces. Even in health care settings that are not teaching hospitals, this positive attitude towards learning is evident, perhaps because of the influence of the hospitals that are affiliated with medical schools.

Another norm in the health care industry relates to ambivalence about bottom-line orientation. As organizations dedicated to providing care, the ethos of many hospitals and nursing homes is more humanitarian than business-like. Several managers cited this when asked why they offered literacy programs. Despite current cost pressures and shifts from not-for-profit to profit centers, many health care organizations consider a caring and compassionate culture as integral to their mission, and managers actively resist market pressures in order to maintain such a culture. Other respondents cited a religious mission that inspired the hospital to care for the poor and could be further enacted through ESL classes. Several hospitals cited their mission or philosophy when explaining why they opened their literacy classes to neighborhood residents and relatives of employees. Yet the conflict between profit and caring becomes a site of struggle. As one manager noted, "Under financial pressure, this might change." Another commented on the changes he had observed:

> I noticed that in the last year a number of hospitals have stopped offering [literacy programs] due to reform and upheaval in health care. This is too bad; it reflects costs, not changes in the labor market. There are still lots of entry level roles at the lower levels. If other organizations are considering implementing such a program, they should figure out a way to legitimize it. They can do it.
>
> *Employment Specialist,*
> *Large Teaching Hospital*

This manager's use of the word "legitimize" adds credence to the assertion that literacy programs are instituted in response to more than just productivity pressures. Furthermore, the admission that hospitals stop offering literacy because of the added costs directly contradicts the rosy rationale about communication skills and employee benefits.

The financial services industry has no such ambivalence about the bottom line. Financial considerations have always been paramount. This may actually inhibit the provision of education, but for image reasons, not the cost of the program. To illustrate: A financial services manager was careful to ascertain the confidentiality of our conversation, since this company did *not* want it widely known that any of its employees were deficient in basic skills. The fear was that customers would lose confidence in the bank, and competitors might attempt to capitalize upon the apparent skill weakness. While it can be argued that public acknowledgment could be particularly damaging in this particular industry, given banks' fiduciary responsibilities, financial services do not differ all that much from other industries in the potential negative impact of an illiterate worker. Nonetheless, this anecdote does suggest that the literacy problem in the workplace may be even greater than is known, and that companies as well as individuals may carry the stigma. Reputation matters, and the legitimacy offered by the education solution is not universally embraced.

With respect to legitimacy, conclusions are paradoxical at this industry level. In both cases described above, laws and certifying standards are so vaguely worded as to result in idiosyncratic interpretations, showing the limits of their determinative power and the extent of managerial discretion. At the same time, the programs can potentially *delegitimize* the organization, as in the example from the bank. It is certainly possible that attempts to alleviate illiteracy in a hospital setting could have similarly delegitimizing consequences. Yet these two industries perhaps place a premium on moral legitimacy: in banking, the fiduciary relationship, and in health, the expectation of care. Consequently, health care and financial services managers face added pressures when making decisions about workplace literacy programs, and they must weigh competing public perceptions. When asked "why the new schoolhouse?" they may not be able to articulate these conflicting pressures, just as they are unable to use costs as a rationale. Their public statements therefore rely upon values and beliefs ("education is good") rather than focusing on the customer ramifications of skill deficiencies.

Demands from the Community and the Students

Community-based adult literacy programs and students themselves exert pressures that are more immediate than the pressures from industry, the state, or the culture. Compared with workplace literacy programs, community-based literacy education programs have a stable mission yet fragile funding stream, and therefore exert influence that is uneven. Adult education programs based in the community are affiliated with social service agencies, community colleges, churches, or public schools—organizations that have education and individual betterment as a key aspect of their mission. There is little ambivalence about this mission: literate adults are the goal, not necessarily productive or compliant workers. The main desired outcome may be to place the adult learners into training programs or jobs, but the work readiness aspects of the literacy curriculum are balanced by learning life skills, related primarily to parenting and citizenship. These programs have survived philosophical shifts and changes in teaching methods over the years with their educational, individual development goals intact. So community-based programs do not face the concern about purpose and responsibility so problematic in discussions of workplace programs, and can endure because their goals are clear. This clarity offers legitimacy to the community programs, and workplace programs in search of legitimacy will mirror their design.

Yet fiscal uncertainties threaten community-based literacy education. Public and nonprofit funding is usual, though funding levels and sources may vary, subject to legislative/political whim. The fragility of community programs is derived from the fact that they are fully dependent on public funding and volunteer efforts. In this era of the declining state and shrinking voluntary sector, this dependence is problematic. This fragility becomes an institutional force: the instability of funding for community-based programs puts added pressures on the private sector to take on this responsibility.

At the same time, institutional pressure can be recognized in the students themselves and their conflicting expectations about schooling. Here the pressure affects the *form* of the workplace program, not the organization's decision to sponsor onsite education. The strong influence of the traditional system of education is evident, as students either want their workplace programs to mirror "real" school, or, conversely, they want these programs to be nothing like "real" school. A few training directors reported making explicit efforts to differentiate the learning experience at work from that of the traditional school. In keeping with one branch of adult education philosophy, they explained that terms such as *teacher, classroom, test,* and *homework* are avoided in order to entice the learner who had not had a positive experience in earlier education. For the most part, though, the managers interviewed were not concerned with semantics and setting, since their employees wanted to replicate the schooling experience they had missed.[17] In fact, the students were leery of nontraditional teaching styles and practices, and reportedly wanted a teacher that "acts like a teacher." Whether their background is one of prior school failure or the fact that earlier education was completed in a country other than the U.S., these students desired the legitimacy of the typical classroom set-up. They requested books, notes, and homework, as well as grades and rigorous evaluations.

This desire to mimic the schooling model indicates the seriousness with which many of the students regard their educational opportunity, since it seems to be the trappings of the educational experience that the students are seeking, as much as knowledge. Managers and teachers respect the learners' preferences for a school-like experience because adult education philosophy suggests that learners themselves know best about how they are to learn and work. One manager stated that "people need the human factor," an observation echoed in the andragogy philosophy. It is interesting to note that several firms experimented with computer assisted instruction for basic skills, but found that this approach worked only as a supplement to a more traditional classroom set-up. Students resisted the novel approach, and again the resistance was taken seriously. Thus students assure that the "schooling model" persists, and education within the new schoolhouse will be little different than education in the old schoolhouse. (See Chapter Four for additional description.)

Community-based literacy programs and adult learners combine to influence the persistence, form, and content of workplace literacy programs. This influence results in pragmatic legitimacy, defined as support for an organization's policy based on its expected value to a variety of constituents (Suchman 1995:578). Yet this is tempered support. Potential students and community practitioners believe that workplace literacy is most legitimate when it is structured like school in the broader culture, rather than an employer-influenced type of schooling. That is, they also want the moral legitimacy enjoyed by education in American culture. Again we see the power of the education ideology as it confronts private sector demands.

Professional Tensions

Students are not the only constituents who want "real school" rather than some vaguely defined corporate version. Adult educators, too, resist organizational limitations of their role, and influence the form that literacy programs take in the workplace. As professionals, they exert normative pressures on organizations, as theories of institutional isomorphism suggest. These professional norms (introduced in Chapter Two) revolve around participation and creating a learner-centered classroom experience. And within the classroom, the educators are for the most part in control—this is where their jurisdiction is made manifest. Yet tension still exists. The educators must negotiate corporate expectations, not only because they are employed by the organization, but also because their professional status has yet to fully consolidate. Consequently, the educators end up both resisting and accommodating business demands, and the resulting tension contributes to the legitimacy of workplace education. Several examples will illustrate.

A newsletter for adult educators published an essay entitled, "The Birds and the Crocodile: A Story of Adult Education." The author wrote that she "realized that creatures that appear to be complete enemies can work together in ways that will benefit them both." She compared the birds who cleaned the crocodiles' teeth to the "two fields once thought to be polar opposites—education and business," concluding that this polarization was unnecessary and harmful to the profession and the students.[18] This article generated heated response, indicating the significance of the conflict and its unresolved nature. The conflict creates a legitimacy management challenge to firms that sponsor workplace education, yet it eventually can work to their advantage. Because the mutual dependence illustrated by the crocodile bird does not involve either dominance or capitulation, educators are heartened in their resistance, at the same time as they are willing to accommodate certain business demands.

The mutual dependence is not without tension, and the following scenario shows how reluctant the accommodation may be. The Massachusetts Workplace Education Consortium brought together employers and funders of workplace literacy programs, with the philosophical goal of encouraging knowledge of each participant's unique perspective, and the pragmatic goal of sharing best practices. The Consortium meetings gave faces to the "state" and the "private sector" and offered a forum for incipient conflicts between and among educators, employers, and state bureaucrats. One budget discussion brought this tension to the fore. The group was hearing a presentation on new fiscal guidelines for workplace programs, and seated near me was the teacher at a hospital-based literacy program, a woman with years of prior experience in community-based literacy education. She whispered, "Do you have any idea how many community slots this [money allotted for workplace literacy] would fund?" The implication was that the workplace programs were receiving a disproportionate amount of resources, and that the money could be better spent elsewhere, on those who were perhaps unemployed due to the paucity of their communication skills. Paradoxically, this disproportionate allocation increased the legitimacy accorded to workplace programs even as it kindled resentment. The state acquiesced to the demands of the private sector, and educators were left to mediate the inequities.

The simultaneous resistance and accommodation of adult educators to corporate expectations serves to further the professionalization process of the educators. They are forced to exhibit their professional expertise even as they learn to speak the language of business interests. Such professional influence was evident in a number of firms studied, where the literacy educators approached the employers (rather than the other way around). The adult educators not only pitched their services as grant writers and as skilled teachers, but also introduced managers to the possibility that literacy might be a problem with their workers. Often this was the first time that the employers had thought seriously about the literacy needs of the workforce. The influence works both ways. Some teachers "go corporate"—adopting the professional demeanor and elite expectations of the corporate world, an association that offers legitimacy and cachet. This is understandable, despite teachers' philosophical unease, because employer-sponsored programs present material advantages, often paying better and involving pleasant and professional working conditions (compare the conference rooms of a high tech company to the church basements where many literacy classes occur). The teachers can be thought of as signaling, "Look, we must be legitimate if businesses are willing to hire us," and employers indicate, "We are legitimate since we consult experts; these professionals share our concerns." The image of the crocodile bird is again illustrative. In attempting to legitimize their occupation as a profession, the teachers assist in the legitimization of the employer-sponsored literacy programs, as each uses the other to persist and thrive.

In conclusion, institutional pressures assist in explaining the phenomenon of workplace literacy programs. First, the persistence of these programs (despite a dearth of evidence as to their efficacy—the subject of the next chapter) is less puzzling after taking into account the educational ideology and the professionalization project of adult educators. Second, the multiple and contradictory nature of managers' justifications is better understood after considering the vague and contradictory forces in the regulatory and industry environments. And third, managerial beliefs about education can be explained by the desire for moral legitimacy. The question "why the new schoolhouse?" continues to defy a simple answer, but the complexity of the responses is less perplexing.

WHY THE NEW SCHOOLHOUSE? THE EMBEDDEDNESS OF EXPLANATION

This chapter has addressed the question of why employers sponsor literacy education, suggesting that there are various explanations, not all evident to the participants themselves. By attending to the explanations offered by the managers, we learn a great deal about the meaning these programs hold. Educational reasons are only part of the answer. Managers want to retain their existing workforce, yet need the imprimatur of the education solution in order to make this appear to be a rational strategy in an external environment that rewards the appearance of high skills and flexible organizations. Furthermore, managers want to work for humane organizations, so they use education to convince themselves that this is so. As to whether workplaces *should* be responsible for education, there is little consensus. The range of responses is instructive: vestiges of paternalism are evident, as is the belief that the public sector is incapable of performing its basic role, and the idea that public responsibilities need collaborative resolutions. Also noteworthy is the absence of economistic logic when managers explain their decision to offer literacy at work. Values and beliefs are apparent in the voices heard, and the managers' explanations are embedded in organizational, industrial, and national cultures.

This embeddedness is even more evident when external, often unarticulated, pressures are taken into account. The institutional perspective adds several layers to our understanding of why some firms select the educational strategy. Organizational and professional legitimacy are important goals, perhaps as important as the ability of the individual to read or the firm to increase productivity. Clearly this is contested terrain, with symbolic and conflictual meanings for firms, teachers, and managers. The next chapter will examine the literacy classroom itself, so as to determine the experience of the learners amidst all the other meanings, and to understand the consequences of employer-sponsored literacy education.

NOTES

1. According to data from the National Organizations Study, neither size, unionization, nor workforce composition has been found to be a predictor for overall training investment, while complex market environments and elaborate internal labor structures do result in more extensive training. See two pieces by David Knoke and Arne Kalleberg, "Job Training in U.S. Organizations," *American Sociological Review* 59 (1994): 537-546, and a different analysis though the same title, the chapter "Job Training in U.S. Organizations," *Organizations in America: Analyzing Their Structures and Human Resource Practices,* edited by Kalleberg et al. (Thousand Oaks: Sage, 1996), 157-179. Training trends and statistics do not necessarily apply to literacy education, though the yearly statistics from *Training Magazine* show a correlation between organizations that do a significant amount of training, and provision of literacy.

2. In the rational world of managerial decision-making, internal and external factors presumably shape company policies: strategic decisions take into account production technologies, workforce capabilities, and market forces. Therefore, an employer's decision to offer literacy education should be a thoughtful response to such factors, and companies with similar combinations of technology and labor might similarly select an "education strategy." The reality is not so straightforward, however. Michael Useem analyzed data collected for a Harris Laborforce 2000 survey, and found it difficult to characterize which types of companies decide to invest in onsite literacy programs, though tentative conclusions were derived. One study found that companies that invested in basic skills tended to be medium sized, have a majority of blue collar workers, and have change-averse management cultures. See Chapter 4, "Company Policies on Education and Training," in *Building the Competitive Workforce,* edited by Philip H. Mirvis

(New York: John Wiley and Sons, 1993). These correlations were statistically significant, but by no means fully explained the decision, since so many companies with these three characteristics do *not* choose to invest in literacy education. According to other research, companies that do not offer literacy education most likely do not define a skills gap as part of their competitive challenge, though they may in fact face similar external pressures as the companies that do offer literacy education. Bassi found that within her sets of matched firms, those with and without education programs appeared quite similar. She concluded that the perception of skill deficiencies is both the cause and the result of having education within the firm. See Laurie J. Bassi, "Workplace Education for Hourly Workers," *Journal of Policy Analysis and Management* 13, no.1 (1994): 55-74.

3. These findings from the manager interviews should be considered illustrative rather than definitive, given the sample size and research methodology. The interviewees were selected from three sectors: manufacturing, health care, and services not related to health care. Firm sizes ranged from medium to large. All were located in Massachusetts. In each firm, I asked to speak with the manager most directly responsible for the literacy program. Their titles varied, with most in the human resources/training departments and a few with operational responsibility. Genders were evenly split.

4. Hollenbeck (1993:31) asked fourteen manufacturing firms why they started workplace education programs, using a forced choice questionnaire. The highest number of "yes" answers were to "employee well-being." The next most frequently noted responses were related to customers and skills. Using a different methodology, he concluded that the existence of a subsidy (i.e., government funding) was a significant factor (77). Bassi also surveyed firms about their motivations. Findings in order of frequency include: to reduce errors and waste; as a benefit to workers (particularly in nonmanufacturing firms); because a subsidy became available; pressure from customers; needed as a result of changes in production; part of a transformation of corporate culture (especially in manufacturing firms); and because it was required by customers (1994:71). What is notable in both studies is that the frequently cited motives—employee well- being, error, and waste reduction—were not necessarily related to education.

5. From a theoretical perspective, this rationale might be considered as exemplifying the resource dependence strand of thinking about organizational behavior. The resource dependence view argues that firms will incorporate new ideas in a logical manner in order to increase organizational effectiveness and efficiency. Organizations act as they do because they are dependent upon various resources to accomplish their goals; in the case at hand, the resource needed is the educated worker, and one rational response is the decision to sponsor literacy classes. Jeffrey Pfeffer and Gerald R. Salancik are the chief articulators of this theory. See *The External Control of Organizations: A Resource Dependence Perspective* (New York: Harper and Row, 1978). The rationality of the resource dependence view is challenged by institutional theory, to be described in the latter half of the chapter.

6. This value orientation is perhaps expected in the health care industry. Unlike manufacturers, health care firms do not have the alternative of going offshore, since their main business involves personal care and they must rely upon people in geographic proximity. Yet contrary to the expectation that literacy is needed by health care workers so that they can communicate effectively and learn to use technology, the hospitals in my small sample most often justifed the educational strategy as a benefit for workers.

7. Jerome L. Himmelstein, *Looking Good and Doing Good: Corporate Philanthropy and Corporate Power* (Bloomington, IN: Indiana University Press, 1997) addresses this issue as he tries to understand philanthropic practices. In asking why the political Right was so often critical of philanthropic practices, ironic because business is ostensibly on the side of political conservatives, he found that executives were more

likely to give money away for reasons that helped the business in a pragmatic sense rather than for any philosophical reasons. The author argues for a pervasive and persuasive corporate pragmatism, which explains the power of big business in American society in a way that transcends politics and ideologies.

8. For more on the relationship between strategy and legitimacy, see Mark C. Suchman's review, "Managing Legitimacy: Strategic and Institutional Approaches," *Academy of Management Review* 20 (1995): 571-610. This chapter will rely on his categorizations of moral and pragmatic legitimacy to assess the influence of external forces.

9. The award-winning article by Sandra Waddock and Samuel Graves is a good source for this assertion, though many have taken on the subject. They write that corporate social performance benefits from and contributes to strong bottom line results, leading to a "virtuous circle." See "The Corporate Social Performance—Financial Performance Link," *Strategic Management Journal*, 18, no.4 (1997): 303-319.

10. These factors were derived from the three sources of isomorphic pressure (mimetic, coercive, and normative) described by Paul DiMaggio and Walter W. Powell, "The Iron Cage Revisited: Institutional Isomorphism and Collective Rationality in Organizational Fields," *American Sociological Review* (April 1983): 147-160.

11. As pointed out by Suchman (1995), the foundational work on legitimacy was done by Weber and Parsons. Many organizational researchers have dealt with it since; his article provides a synthesis, comparing and contrasting institutional and strategic approaches.

12. The idea that organizations are influenced by what can be considered non-rational (i.e., myth-like) factors is the key tenet of institutional theory. For one of the earliest works on the topic, see John W. Meyer and Brian Rowan, "Institutionalized Organizations: Formal Structure as Myth and Ceremony," *American Journal of Sociology* 83 (1977): 340-363. Another book, Walter W. Powell and Paul J. DiMaggio, eds., *The New Institutionalism in Organizational Analysis* (Chicago: University of Chicago Press, 1991) offers an assessment of institutional theory, a compilation of critical articles and chapters, and a wonderfully inclusive bibliography.

13. A study by institutionalists Scott and Meyer concluded that training within nonschool organizations had become more school-like because of the widespread acceptance of the traditional models of instruction. W. Richard Scott and John M. Meyer, "The Rise of Training Programs in Firms and Agencies: An Institutional Perspective," *Research in Organizational Behavior* 13 (Greenwich, CT: JAI Press, 1991): 297-326.

14. *Workforce 2000* and its accompanying publicity have since been critiqued in the academic press. The study garnered such attention because of its widespread misinterpretation, its faulty methodology, and the assumptions about corporate practices and public policies on which it was based. See Roy A. Teixeira and Lawrence Mishel, "Skills Shortage or Management Shortage?" in *The New Modern Times,* edited by David B. Bills (Albany: State University of New York Press, 1995), 193-205, and the article by Nancy DiTomaso and Judith J. Friedman, "A Sociological Commentary on Workforce 2000," also in *The New Modern Times,* 207-233. Whatever its flaws, *Workforce 2000* resonated with managerial concerns to the extent that it was used by some to justify investment in literacy classes.

15. This phrase, and other ideas concerning moral legitimacy are from Suchman (1995:579).

16. Obviously this attempt at understating the industry-specific pressures at work is limited given the scope and intent of this study. Other researchers have looked at sector, rather than industry, in efforts to explain patterns of literacy program adoption. Their findings are inconsistent, yet still instructive with respect to the connection (or lack

thereof) between skills and knowledge, and educational programs. See bibliographic references for Chisman (1992), Bassi (1992), Useem (1993), Hollenbeck (1993).

17. This phenomenon extends beyond the workplace. In discussing the nontraditional student, Kett, in *The Pursuit of Knowledge Under Difficulties* (1994) writes, "To an extent that has dismayed veteran adult educators, many of these older students have sought carbon copies of the education afforded their younger counterparts" (p.xviii).

18. *all write news* 10, no. 5 (Boston: Adult Literacy Resource Institute, March/April 1994):1, 4. Subsequent letters criticized the premises and the analysis, challenging the dichotomous thinking and the lack of a structural perspective that sees business blaming labor for educational deficiencies when the larger economic relations need to be called into question. These are useful criticisms of the business/education tension, and the structural perspective is addressed again in the concluding chapter.

Learning to Be Literate at Work: Rhetoric and Reality

Employer-sponsored literacy programs are used by companies to address a range of concerns, some clearly educational, others less so. Legitimacy appears at least as important as literacy when a work organization takes on the responsibility of basic skills education. Workplace literacy programs assuredly carry significant *symbolic* value, to participants and to the external environment. Thus far, the discussion has focused on context: cultural beliefs about the value of education, various interpretations of the adult illiteracy problem, and the organizational and environmental influences on managers as they justify literacy education in the workplace. Beyond this, what actually occurs inside the literacy classroom? This chapter will describe curriculum materials, teaching methods, time allotments, enrollment practices, teacher characteristics, and types of students, allowing the "new schoolhouse" label to be more fully assessed. I will continue to consider the consequences of employer responsibility by examining control of educational content, support for students, teacher autonomy, and unspoken curriculum messages. Managers' voices begin the discussion, as they take on the debates about purpose and benefit.

THE WORKPLACE CLASSROOM: BALANCING INTERESTS

I expected to find that workplace literacy programs would be narrowly tailored to work tasks, with organizational goals paramount. This expectation originated with my own experience of allegedly "teaching them too much": I thought employers would try to limit what was being taught, and that the curriculum would be narrow and designed to benefit the organization. Human capital theory and its assertion that employers will not invest in general skills back up this hypothesis, as does the functional context method of teaching.[1] Furthermore, the business literature advocates a tailored curriculum design. But managers' responses were not as anticipated—a summary of their answers shows that the majority of workplace literacy programs are broadly educative in design and methodology, and attempt to meet both organizational and individual needs. Twenty-four managers were asked, "what is the curriculum like?" and were probed about its connection with work skills. Nearly half of the managers reported a design that addressed work and nonwork topics. Six managers described curricula that were definitely not work related. On the other hand, four respondents answered that they were trying to assure that learning *was* limited to work-related topics. Several had no knowledge of the curriculum, a significant finding in and of itself. These numbers indicate a salient diversity in approach, and a tilt towards the broadly designed curriculum. Managers' comments reveal their awareness of the design options, and varied rationales for their decisions:

> We tied it to work to make it meaningful, but didn't want to limit it to that [i.e. work related]. Definitely a well-rounded program that also dealt with personal life, the daily routine, etc.
>
> *Senior Training Representative,*
> *Large Financial Services Organization*

> We didn't want it exclusively tied to work. We were afraid they would just memorize the forms, not really learn to read them.
>
> *Training Director,*
> *Community Hospital*

These quotes show that the managers were aware of the tug between learning designed for personal benefit and that which was work-related. Although learner needs reportedly predominate, organizational benefits are not ignored. The attention to progressive definitions of learning is notable: the program was not narrowly designed because of a desire to be "well-rounded" and to preclude memorization.

What was also striking about these curriculum decisions was the fact that they were not fixed, and in several cases appeared all but experimental. Curriculum was modified in response to feedback from participants. One of the firms discontinued its narrowly focused approach after a year, since there were so many complaints from learners and teachers. To quote:

> We began using company forms. Neither the students nor teachers liked it, so we gave them what they wanted. Now, this is just learning, not forms and procedures.
>
> *Human Resource Manager,*
> *Mid-sized Retail Distribution Company*

Along the same lines, one manager reported that the materials used in the students' jobs were not complex enough. "There is only so much reading that a janitor has to do," she said. So her company adopted a standardized adult education text that was not work-specific. Another organization attempted to move in the opposite direction:

> We started broad, now we are trying to narrow. After meeting students' needs for three and a half years, we are now trying to address business needs.
>
> *Human Resources Director,*
> *Mid-sized Manufacturer*

In this firm, the question of changing the design had created tension within the planning committee and among the students:

> We wanted a new job-specific class; we didn't want to start teaching people grammar but rather safety on rubber molding. But we took into account that you'd have to back way up and start with vocabulary. It's starting now, [we are] not sure what it will look like. We are working with a consultant who is doing the [job-task] evaluation and we have a planning and evaluation committee. But the group hasn't clicked. They are going on two prongs. One is work-specific: teach people reflectively how to do the job, not just how to press the button, so if the supervisor is not here, they can figure out for themselves. Concurrently, go forward with the basic skill component—math and language—so that people have the foundation to continue to take other training.
>
> But there is a real split in the group. Some people that are more visionary and feel that we should be laying the groundwork and there are others that feel that we've been doing this English class for four to five years and "we just need people who know how to do their jobs, godammit." And the employees are sort of split that way too, the better-educated people may already know how to do fractions, actually, the better-educated people are more visionary. Others want no more classrooms, just hands-on.

This disagreement about the design of the next phase highlights two educational truisms: first, the importance of foundational competency as a precursor to job-specific learning, particularly if the goal is that the learner understand the task fully, "not just how to press the button"; and second, that true literacy gains are time consuming, whether basic skills or English language acquisition, and require a long-term commitment on the part of the organization as well as the individual learner. Meanwhile, as job demands escalate and both learners and their supervisors tire of the classes, "visionary" goals becoming secondary to productivity. The manager saw an obvious split in the group, and was uncertain how to proceed. An educator would have few doubts about these issues, since educators accept that learning takes time, and learning design should be cumulative. These truisms, of course, are difficult to enact in business organizations, and thus we uncover one of the key lessons of the new schoolhouse: organizations must take their educational responsibility seriously if they are to increase literacy skills and assure transference to work tasks. This means becoming more like school, in terms of time allotted to learning and the curriculum sequence.

Among those who decided not to emphasize work-related materials at all in their curricular designs, most agreed with the above philosophy that the workers had to learn English first, and accepted that language learning classes were necessarily broad in focus. They anticipated a narrower focus in the future. Yet this was not always the case. One firm had no clear anticipation of either organizational gain or change over time. "This is for them," one explained. And as for the four respondents who answered that they were trying to assure that learning *was* limited to work-related topics, a typical answer was: "All is work-oriented. We did the job-task analyses—there are no life skills taught." Clearly this manager was aware of other possible curricular foci (e.g., "life skills") but had decided to orient the lessons to the demands of the workplace. There is support for this technique, "job-task analysis," as well as for this philosophical approach, as will be described below.

Why such inconsistent responses, and why such divergence from expectations? Several explanations are possible. The influence of the adult educators is a significant factor in explaining the propensity towards a broad, learner-centered curriculum. Their influence is evident elsewhere, in the handful of managers that said that they had no idea what the curriculum covered. These managers reported that they left such decisions to the teachers, a fact that may be welcomed by the teachers attempting to further their professionalization project, yet a finding that challenges expectations of employer control. However, the adult educators are by no means an absolute force: organizational demands and their own professional schisms restrict their power. Finally, policy makers as well as educators may influence managers' decisions.

Official and Expert Perspectives on the Workplace Curriculum

Clearly there is a tension in the workplace between a learning design that is job-specific and that which is more general, and this tension is acknowledged and negotiated by those directly responsible for workplace literacy—managers and teachers. The tension is evident at other levels, as well. Public sector policy makers and the adult education establishment have been active in the curricular debate, though their influence is uneven, since outside experts themselves disagree and politics interferes. Nonetheless, these official rationales are echoed in the managers' varied rhetoric.

Exhortatory policy statements reveal predictable positions on the issue of broad versus narrow curriculum. From the business perspective, the 1999 Conference Board report on workplace literacy, *Turning Skills into Profit,* states that "such programs are often customized to meet specific workplace needs" (Bloom and Lafleur 1999:4). While this seems a straightforward suggestion that organizational goals should drive design, "customized" can be defined otherwise, as meeting learner needs rather than workplace needs. *Equipped for the Future,* a policy report published by the National Institute for Literacy in 1997, advocates that content be "customer-driven, shaped by what adults say they need to know to succeed in our brave new world" (9). This is the "learner-centered" model, familiar to the adult education establishment. Content guidelines are less theoretical in requests for proposals: some, though not all, state-funded programs require that learners be involved in curriculum development. If organized labor is involved, the program design can be deliberately critical, advocating what might be considered anti-organizational topics: worker rights, labor history, etc.[2] However, to the dismay of the radical adult educators, the critical literacy approach is often tempered by the reality of the learner-centered philosophy—students do not necessarily want to raise their consciousness or to learn of the failings of capitalism; rather, they want to better their own options without challenging the system.[3]

Formal evaluation research ostensibly avoids the political considerations of the various constituents considered above. Such studies confirm what most managers conclude: curriculum should be balanced between individual and organizational needs, and should be neither exclusively broad nor exclusively narrow. Forrest Chisman compiled results from other researchers nationwide.[4] He found that employers benefit most from the provision of general, broad-based education that is not necessarily customized but consists of "fairly standard adult education curricula." His rationale is surprising, however. He suggests that such curricula are nearly always found in conjunction with other workplace changes. He writes, "Building new sets of relationships between management and workers and new attitudes towards work is at least as important an aim and benefit [as new skills and knowledge]" (88). So perhaps "turning skills into profit" involves more than simply a customized literacy program; for purposes here, suffice it to say that his review of the research comes out on the side of breadth, and, again counterintuitively, breadth is thought to result in greater *employer* benefit. Thus a balanced curriculum is the recommendation of scholarly researchers because it is thought to have optimal benefits for both organizations and individuals. Teaching methods and materials are also important, and controversial.

Classroom Climate and Learning Texts

An interesting twist to the curriculum debate is brought about by educators and cognitive psychologists who sidestep the purpose and benefit questions to ask, "how do adults learn best?" Again, definitive answers are elusive, with consensus on classroom climate but debate about the texts to be used.

Adults and those who educate them are generally in agreement that a participatory classroom atmosphere is most conducive to learning, whether in the community or in the workplace. Teachers do not lecture, rather, they engage students in discussion and activities related to jointly selected topics; this is the crux of a learner-centered design. The trappings of authority are minimized, as are rewards and punishments. The assumption is that students come motivated to learn and will progress as rapidly as they are able. Teachers believe that students should be allowed to move at their own pace, and in some instances select their own topics. Tests are given, though in most workplaces the emphasis is less on standardized performance than on individual progress. There is a positive tone to student/teacher interactions, and this is clearly an environment where different learning styles and different cultures are respected.

However, there is ongoing disagreement in the adult education field concerning the extent to which classroom materials should be tied to work tasks. On one extreme are those who believe that classes should be taught using general, classic texts and should remain relatively free of organization-specific themes, eschewing work skills entirely. (This view is not limited to educators—recall the manager quoted in the discussion of employer responsibility who spoke of Yeats and Keats.) Advocates of this perspective suggest that the skills learned in this manner will be transferable outside of the workplace, and may result in critical consciousness.[5] This is the curricular foundation of liberal education, and is highly valued yet disproportionately allocated, as described in the first chapter.

Opposing this view are those who suggest that adults learn best in an applied, experiential manner, and therefore that work activities provide the ideal "text" from which to teach basic skills. This technique, one version of which is called the "functional context method" (Sticht, *Literacy at Work,* 1991), recommends that students be taught basic skills using actual contexts (forms, manuals, memos) that they encounter on the job. The functional context method is controversial, however, for reasons both economic and educational. The economic argument has two distinct prongs: first, transferability of skills is increasingly desired in the dynamic economy because of the rapid changes in jobs and work conditions; and second, context-dependent curriculum development can be costly. One researcher in the field writes:

> It is quite possible to develop a functional literacy curriculum for the learner's specific occupational role in a specific place of employment. Yet given the great diversity of role and setting, this approach to literacy is expensive and time consuming and learners may find it difficult to generalize beyond the workplace and the literacy skills learned. (Beder 1991:5)

From this perspective, generalizability is of interest for purposes of the newly desired "flexible" workplace, and may be considered a long-term rather than a short-term investment that, in turn, may require the visionary management and open-minded students described earlier. The criticism is that a narrow approach like the functional context method, though it can result in literacy and productivity, may be overly technocratic, and therefore unable to prepare employees for the future high performance workplace, with its demands of continual learning and flexibility.[6]

As for the cost argument, it becomes another "make" or "buy" type of decision, and making an employer-tailored literacy course can be surprisingly expensive. Those unfamiliar with the complexities of the curriculum development process often resist paying teachers and staff for the preparation time necessary. Furthermore, such a process would have to be regularly repeated as work tasks changed. In this regard, it may not be surprising that the functional context method is most commonly used in the predictable environment of the military, with its clear roles and rules. A truly tailored curriculum is expensive. However, since none of the employers in my study reported doing any sort of cost benefit analysis, and few spoke about their workplace literacy programs in calculable terms, the rationality of these economic explanations must be viewed with some skepticism. Less rational, noneconomic explanations must also be considered.

Along those lines, as the earlier quotes established, teachers have found that students are apt to protest against the functional, narrow methods: their work contexts are often not stimulating enough to hold their interest and teach them what they need to know. Therefore, in most cases, the adult education establishment has convinced employers that the purchased curricula, broad in scope, are equally as useful, and perhaps more beneficial in the long run. This is not to say that an off-the-shelf workbook ignores employer-specific concerns. Rather, the curriculum integrates experience into the design—built upon the participation of the learners, as adult education philosophy suggests. Therefore, learning activities emerge from the class, a less-expensive way to assure that there is a work connection, yet with learners, not employers, determining the topic. This method also takes into account the fact that individual learning styles differ, and an adaptable learning design that includes a range of types of texts may be most appropriate.

Taking their classroom experiences as well as their philosophies into account, most teachers are found somewhere in the middle between the liberal (classical) educators and those who support the functional context method.[7] As dedicated professionals, they want to teach in ways that adults learn best. These teachers do not want their lessons to be confined to narrow job tasks, but they do want to use teaching materials that are important to their students' lives, including but not limited to their work. Therefore, teachers advocate the use of materials based on relevant topics such as work, health, and citizenship. Educators are used to working in an environment where resources are constrained, so their solution may again be as much pragmatic as ideological. Still, their ideals are supported by a wide range of published materials, pertaining to real world issues such as driver education, communication with children's teachers and doctors, citizenship laws, money management, and so forth. While this may not be Shakespeare, neither is it reading mopping instructions. Such a compromise is acceptable to most educators.

Published curriculum materials typically take a balanced approach to the question of breadth, and add legitimacy to the decision to avoid an overly tailored approach. A large proportion of these books and activities relate to work life in general, including cognitive and social skills, vocational exploration, organizational dynamics, and labor literacy. And formal efforts are ongoing among ESL teachers to create a work-oriented curriculum. Titles tell the story: "English for Special Purposes," "English as a Working Language," "English that Works." Such lessons are designed for community settings as well as workplaces, since much that happens in the community is concerned with preparing the learner for employment. A recent innovation, gaining attention from educators and employers alike, is the metacognitive approach, which one publisher calls "Learning to Learn." Learning to Learn is taught through eliciting a "real" problem from students, then taking them through a prescribed critical thinking method. The key is to make cognitive processes visible (e.g., "divide the problem into parts," "look at your resources"). The skilled workplace educator will elicit work problems as well as personal problems for discussion. Employers and workers alike benefit from such an emphasis, and the method is both job-specific and generalizable. What is also noteworthy is the participatory nature of the learning design.

In summary, the adult educators have a high degree of autonomy inside the classroom, and the practice of most in the adult education field is to teach adults the skills they need, using materials that are neither narrowly job-specific nor so unrelated as to be unduly abstract, in a manner that is interactive and participatory. It should be repeated that the students, who want the familiar school trappings of authority, homework, and teacher-directed learning, do not always welcome this participatory model, but skilled teachers expect this resistance and gradually convince the students of the value of the adult, learner-centered model. Some employers resist this recommendation, too, believing that their organization will benefit most from learning that is job-specific and/or traditionally didactic, but the majority of employer-sponsored programs either find a broad enough curriculum to balance individual and organizational interests, or tend towards simply meeting the individual worker needs with a curriculum that is "for them." The fact that managers have adopted a broad approach in most cases may reflect the growing influence of the field of adult education; it may also be an economic decision, since tailored materials are expensive to produce and may not result in the outcome desired. Institutional pressures could also be at work: cultural beliefs about education as well as the professionalization project of the adult educators subtly argue against a narrow definition of learning. The educators appear to have triumphed in the curriculum debate. However, employers find other means to control the learning made available to adults, and to assure that organizational needs remain paramount.

CONSTRAINTS ON LITERACY ATTAINMENT: COMPETING INTERESTS IN THE WORKPLACE

Attention to the nature of the workplace curriculum must be accompanied by an assessment of the time allotted for learning at work, and the types of support made available to students. Both are constrained, leading to the recognition that the learning that occurs may be similarly truncated. Literacy classes typically meet for a few hours a week, most often in fourteen-week semesters, approximating a college model. This alone seems very little, especially compared with the time allotted to teach children the same basic skills. Policy documents continually advocate greater intensity—a minimum of five classroom hours a week.[8] Yet it is difficult for employers to set aside that amount of time, since literacy classes interfere with other organizational priorities, even when such classes are offered on the students' own time. Students can learn outside of class hours, and homework may be assigned; though again, expectations must be minimal, given the myriad time pressures on the adult learners. Time and intensity are challenges faced by community programs as well, yet are exacerbated in the workplace because of the immediacy of the competing pressures and the fact that employees' main organizational responsibility is work, not education.

Even with relatively few hours per week allotted for class, there are still barriers to full participation. Time away from work and compensation are the major topics of concern. Some classes are scheduled during work time, and class attendance is fully paid; other employers pay half time, and classes usually meet partly during work and partly during breaks or lunch; and some employers do not pay at all, no matter the time scheduled. This alone poses a problem for the adult learners, many of whom make little more than minimum wage and typically have one or two other jobs. The training and human resource managers report that their biggest problem is attendance, resulting from production pressures, child care difficulties, transportation troubles, and the time squeeze of second or third jobs, making it difficult to juggle class time after work hours, especially if class time is unpaid. Managers attempt to foster better attendance by meeting with direct supervisors and in some cases offering training for the supervisors themselves, to stress the importance of ongoing education and to help find coverage for the workers during class time. Managers report that they have tried a range of time slots for the classes, and continually experiment with different combinations of paid and unpaid time in order to make it possible for enrollees to attend class. There seems to be no single solution to the scheduling problem, which is chronic also in community-based programs.

Support to attend class is not the only way in which learning is limited. Often, the number of slots available does not meet the demand for literacy, so not all employees that are interested get to attend. Waiting lists are ubiquitous. In some cases, managers deal with the scarcity by rationing the educational opportunity for lower level workers: employees are not allowed to progress to higher levels of education until others have had their turn at attaining basic skills. Other employers add more classes, though this can be difficult to justify given the attendance problems. Typically the employers are content to keep the demand high, so as to justify continued investment and/or maintain interest.

Some employers offer workplace literacy for only a short period of time because they see it as a catalyst. They hope that the workplace experience will inspire students to take advantage of opportunities in the outside educational system. In many large companies, tuition reimbursement programs provide supplemental educational options when employers cease to sponsor onsite learning, yet the lower-level employees find offsite classes even more of a challenge to attend, again for reasons of child care, transportation, and second jobs. Furthermore, tuition reimbursement is usually limited to college-level courses, and the majority of the ESL and adult basic education students have yet to obtain a high school diploma, so they are not eligible.

So the key finding is that employers do not control what is learned, but do constrain the time devoted to learning. The rhetoric of broad educational opportunity is confronted with the reality of limited employer commitment to the educational role. However, such limitations do not mean that learning is thwarted because time is not necessarily the determining element. Other factors influence whether literacy is attained: the teacher plays a crucial role, as do the students themselves. This chapter will continue the task of describing the classroom experience by focusing on these key actors.

ADULT EDUCATORS: PROFESSIONAL POWER IN ACTION

Good teachers are vital, managers asserted with emotion. Often volunteering laudatory remarks before being questioned on the subject, managers offered such accolades as, "the teacher was really able to connect to the students," and "she was the key to the group's motivation." Respondents reported that the success of their programs was attributable to the skill of the teachers, not any particulars of the curriculum:

> Quality staff is the key. The teacher is better this year and attendance is up.
> *Director of Training and Organizational Development,*
> *Large Hospital*

Consequently, teachers are given significant autonomy with respect to workplace literacy. In addition to the obvious classroom duties, they assist in the recruitment of students, do the initial assessments of skills and knowledge, assign students to the appropriate level of instruction, design and implement curriculum, measure outcomes, and evaluate the program. While their expertise in all facets may be necessary, employers use as their main evaluative criteria whether or not the students like the teacher, and they judge this anecdotally and by virtue of class attendance. One high tech manager said, "They (the workers) may not be highly educated, but they surely know the difference between good and bad teaching. And if the teacher is bad, they simply won't go. We hear about it." Once a satisfactory teacher is found, managers allow them the autonomy that befits not only professional expertise, but also popularity. As already described, their active presence legitimizes the organization's efforts with regard to education, while at the same time they keep the workplace programs from becoming dominated by business goals.

Adult educators are also influential because they are organizational outsiders. The majority of the teachers are not company employees, but are contracted through community colleges or independent agencies. In the few instances where the company has an in-house person teach basic skills, this person usually has an education degree and/or experience in technical training. Managers come to realize that they need expertise, and it is usually preferable to "buy" rather than "make" expertise in the field of adult basic skills education, even in firms that have their own training staff. Those who teach in the workplace often have experience teaching in the community prior to coming to the new setting. As outsiders, the teachers bring with them the practices and philosophies prevalent in the community adult education venue, assuring that the curriculum is not overly narrow and that the teaching methodology is inclusive and learner-centered. Experts in the field believe that teaching adults in such a participatory manner requires special skills, and a unique mind set. One community college affiliated workplace education director made this most obvious when she said that she would not hire people who had been teachers in the traditional K-12 system, since she had seen so many "bomb" in the workplace despite their familiarity with the subject matter of basic skill development. She felt that their approach to education was so fundamentally different so as to be insulting to the learners, and she was not very confident of their ability to communicate with the managers either. This clear differentiation is welcomed by those interested in the progress of the adult education field, at the same time as it assures managers that they are getting the appropriate expertise. Learner characteristics also influence the classroom experience.

ADULT LEARNERS: STIGMA AND SPECIAL POPULATIONS

Because of the fragmentation of the employer-based system, demographic data are not routinely collected on literacy program participants.[9] Not surprisingly, workers deemed in need of literacy are typically found in the periphery of the labor market, where women and people of color are highly represented. Since workplace literacy programs are usually limited to full-time permanent employees, many contingent employees are not eligible (though several hospitals in this study allowed part-timers and even family members to attend classes). The largest demographic groups are those who do not speak English as a first language, typically immigrants. Secondary sources confirm that many participants in workplace literacy programs are immigrants who have limited English proficiency, though this is not highlighted in policy or employer rhetoric. In Massachusetts, the majority of workplace education programs teach English as a Second Language (ESL)[10] or, as it is sometimes known, English to Speakers of Other Languages (ESOL). Typically these participants are newly arrived immigrants,[11] though some are long-standing employees who now are thought to need better English skills in order to be successful in the changing workplace. A proportion of these students is not literate in any language, though this is difficult to determine.

Other participants are native English-speaking adults who may have dropped out of school, or simply graduated without ever having obtained basic literacy skills. They can be characterized as ordinary working-class Americans, who have managed to disguise their lack of basic skills by inhabiting dead-end jobs with little chance of movement (Chisman 1989:2). A great deal of stigma in our culture is associated with not being able to read, so this group is especially difficult to identify. One manager reported that employees had lied about having high school diplomas, not to avoid going to class but because of fear of losing their jobs. If they can be persuaded that their illiterate status should be openly addressed, such adults take classes in ABE (adult basic education) where they may be mixed with nonnative speakers who have progressed to the point that they no longer need special second language teaching.

These two groups—immigrants and illiterate native speakers—pose different challenges, particularly at the early stages of a workplace literacy endeavor. Separate classes and usually different teachers are needed for ESL and ABE, and learning materials are unique to each group. With regard to recruitment and student motivation, the ESL students are less stigmatized than the illiterate native speakers, and so are more willing to come to class and likely to be openly enthused about the opportunity. The illiterate native speakers have typically had negative experiences with school, and often have undiagnosed learning disabilities. While they may be open to the opportunity to learn at work, their individual circumstances pose special challenges to the adult educator. Such students often need counseling and one-on-one instruction, neither of which are compatible with the competing pressures of the workplace.

BEYOND RHETORIC

The previous sections sought to describe the practices of the workplace literacy classroom, since the classroom is where philosophical questions are addressed (or ignored), where policies become practice, where cultural beliefs are made obvious, and where institutional forces become manifest. Rhetoric was confronted by reality, and key findings are as follows:

- The curriculum and methods of workplace classrooms tend to be broad and learner-centered, rather than organizationally focused.
- Managers constrain learning in various ways: classes are restricted in time and duration, demand is encouraged but not met, enrollments are limited, managers decide how much education is enough, and support to attend classes is variable.
- Managers rely upon adult educators, who are usually organizational outsiders, to do much of the planning and implementation of the literacy program.

- A significant amount of workplace literacy is for nonnative speaking workers, usually immigrants.

Consequently, the workplace literacy program is much like the community literacy program with respect to materials, methodology, teachers, and students. However, organizations *do* assure that their needs predominate, though not through control of curriculum. Boundaries have been blurred, albeit in unexpected ways. Employers limit the time available for learning, effectively constraining the opportunity to increase literacy. Given this control, vocal concern about the nature of the curriculum serves to obfuscate the minimal impact such programs can have, notwithstanding employer focus or teaching design. The next chapter will build upon this discussion of reality and rhetoric by further assessment of the symbolic and educative consequences of such endeavors.

NOTES

1. The functional context method is attributed to Thomas Sticht, who designed it for use in the military. Its mechanics and associated controversies will be briefly described later in the chapter. See Thomas G. Sticht, *Literacy at Work,* (New York: Simon and Schuster Education Group, 1991), as well as numerous other government reports on the topic, many of which were written by Sticht.

2. An excellent if somewhat polemical critique of the entire subject of workplace literacy is offered by Sheila Collins, "Workplace Literacy: Corporate Tool or Worker Empowerment?" *Social Policy* (Summer 1989): 26-30. The author concludes by advocating strong union involvement in any such program, and believes that the critical labor literacy approach is essential.

3. Paul Willis describes the educational basis of such working class consent in *Learning to Labor: How Working Class Kids Get Working Class Jobs* (New York: Columbia University Press, 1977). A more recent analysis of the complexity of raising critical consciousness is provided by Steven Vallas, *Power in the Workplace* (1993). For a discussion of learner resistance to literacy in the workplace, see the ethnography by Gowen, *The Politics of Workplace Literacy* (1992).

4. In *The Missing Link* (1992) Chisman writes, "Somewhere in America some company is providing basic skills instruction in almost every imaginable way. Differences arise from the fact that workplace education programs are customized to the needs of the employer, workers, and educators who develop them" (24).

5. As advocated by Friere and his followers, described in Chapter Two; for an example, see the curriculum published by New Readers Press, "More Than a Job" (New York: no date or author). This is Frierian-based and takes a critical look at work, the economy, and jobs.

6. Sondra Stein, "Workplace Literacy and the Transformation of the American Workplace: A Model for Effective Practice" (unpublished paper, 1989). Stein's influential ideas about the high performance workplace and the model of adult education needed to bring about such changes were first set forth in this 1989 conference paper. She works for the National Institute for Literacy, as director of Equipped for the Future. Equipped for the Future (EFF) is the National Institute for Literacy's standards-based system reform initiative aimed at improving the quality and outcomes of the adult literacy and lifelong learning delivery system. EFF starts from the recognition that the skills adults need as parents, workers, and citizens go beyond the basic academic skills that have traditionally

been targeted by adult education programs. Several reports have been published as a result of this project. The Executive Summary is provided by Stein in *Equipped for the Future: A Reform Agenda for Adult Literacy and Lifelong Learning* (Washington, DC: National Institute for Literacy: 1997).

7. As part of an ongoing research project, Harvard Graduate School of Education researchers devised a program typology, based on Frierian categories of life-contextualized/decontextualized and dialogic/monologic, and rated several hundred programs along its dimensions. They found most programs were clustered in the middle of both categories; with very few extremes. Researchers believe that this reflects teachers' intentions to address two competing approaches: the need for skills and the need for students to determine their own course of study. See Victoria Purcell-Gates, S. Degener and E. Jacobson *Report #2: Adult Literacy Program Practice: A Typology Across Dimensions of Life-Contextualized/Decontextualized and Dialogic/Monologic* (Cambridge, MA: National Center for the Study of Adult Learning and Literacy, July 1998).

8. Massachusetts Department of Education "Guidelines for Effective Adult Basic Education 2000" are very clear on this subject. Guideline #3 reads, "Programs **must** provide a minimum of 5 hours of instruction up through a maximum of 20 hours of instruction each week, the major portion of which must involve group based instruction, for students enrolled in non-volunteer based instructional services." The rationale offered is: "Unnecessarily low levels of instructional intensity frustrate students and are not cost effective due to the increased need to review 'last week's' lessons. Very high levels of intensity (>20 hrs/wk) generally result in diminished 'return on investment' as the amount of new material an adult can acquire within a week 'plateaus.' " See <http://www.doe.mass.edu/acls/abeguide.htm>

9. The limitations of existing statistics are described by Chisman in *The Missing Link* (1992). From a broader perspective, those who test at the lowest NALS level are disproportionately African Americans or other racial minorities, though these groups do not necessarily receive their share of literacy training at work.

10. In 1993, 81% (of 110) Massachusetts workplace education programs consisted in part or in whole of ESL, and in 1995 both the number and the percentage increased: 101 of 117 workplaces, or 86%. The majority of companies (65%) combined ESL offerings with basic skills (ABE—adult basic education, or GED preparation), though approximately one-third offered ESL only. The cases in my sample mirrored this breakdown exactly, though inadvertently.

11. Immigrants accounted for 60% percent of the labor force growth in the years from 1980 to 1995 in Massachusetts, and nearly half of these had only a high school degree or less. (*Boston Globe*, January 21, 1996, citing Andrew Sum's new study in "The State of the American Dream in New England"). The pace increased in the latter half of the decade. According to research by the Massachusetts Institute for a New Commonwealth (MassINC), more than 80% of labor force growth during the 1990s was due to foreign immigration. Kimberly Blanton, "Study Details Immigrants' Importance" *Boston Globe* (November 17, 1999). Massachusetts is one of the five states most dependent upon immigrant workers.

5

Learning to Be Literate at Work: The Impact on Organizations and Individuals

> It took us about three months to find out that there were some
> unanticipated dividends: these were loyalty and a positive
> view of the company.
>
> *Human Resources Director,*
> *Multi-national Manufacturer*

Expectations are high with respect to the new schoolhouse; consequently, its impact is not trivial and often not as anticipated. General education certainly occurs in work settings, in literacy classes that are broadly construed and much like classes in the community. There is little evidence to substantiate fears of employer domination with regard to curriculum; rather, the educators' learner-centered goals persist. Yet employers constrain learning in significant ways, by allotting little time and minimal support to workers attending literacy classes. Given this, what are the organizational and individual consequences? This chapter will review managers' responses to questions about impact, and will compare these findings to the findings of other researchers. Unacknowledged consequences will also be described, based on analyses of what managers do not mention and the inconsistencies in their comments. I will argue that workplace literacy programs benefit organizations and individuals, and though they threaten to blur the boundaries of private and public responsibility, they actually sustain the status quo and contribute to organizational and institutional stability.

This is a long chapter, in part because managers have so much to say on the subject.

As has been established, employers expect these programs to solve a range of organizational problems, and policy makers envision that social problems will be ameliorated by the workplace literacy classes. Given these multiple and sometimes conflicting aims, it is not surprising that the organization experiences consequences that are "unanticipated," as the manager observes in the quote above. What *is* surprising is the realization that employers are not heavily invested in measurable outcomes or benefits. In most cases, the impacts of the literacy programs are not assessed in any systematic manner. Neither educational gains nor organizational benefits are quantified, rather, the efficacy of the workplace literacy program seems to be taken on faith and anecdote. This can be understood in part by the value placed on education in U.S. society, yet that factor alone does not adequately explain the continuation of the employer-sponsored educational efforts. This finding brings renewed attention to the symbolic value of the programs, and to the fact that educational outcomes are only a small part of the motivation for investing in literacy. Again, perceptions are as important as actuality.

THE CHALLENGE OF MEASURING PROGRAM IMPACT

From a pragmatic perspective, the question about program outcomes is the most fundamental one that can be asked about employer-sponsored education, especially given the high expectations: one would expect that managers and policy makers alike would be curious about results, raising such evaluative questions as "Are these programs effective?" and "Do some models work better than others?" Managers who have been charged with implementing employer-sponsored education programs are presumably accountable to the supervisors who have released the employees to attend class, as well as to senior executives who have approved the expenditure and endorsed the strategic direction of human capital investment. Policy makers, too, must answer to constituents who are interested in how tax dollars are spent, and to literacy advocates who wonder about sharing responsibility with the private sector. Yet measurement is a challenge—both individual and organizational outcomes are admittedly difficult to assess.

This measurement difficulty is inherent in the educational activity itself. In order for education to happen, the teacher must teach, but more importantly the learner must learn—and learning is an internal cognitive process beyond the control of the teacher or manager. Outcomes vary independently of input, making true assessment a challenge. Testing is the usual mechanism for measuring learning gains, though tests are problematic for adult learners because so many of them have test anxiety and such poor skills to begin with. Testing reveals who does well on tests, and while tests may be diagnostically useful, illiterate adults often resist or are incapable of completion. At their best, tests may allow assessment of individual learning gains—organizational effects are even more difficult to determine.[1] Short of rigidly controlled experimental design, it is difficult to assess educational outcomes with much reliability and/or validity because there are so many intervening variables.

Knowing this, the decision was made to ask managers about outcomes in an open-ended manner. I hypothesized that their ability or inability to acknowledge the inherent difficulty of the task would offer clues to the meanings that they had associated with education in their organization. To reiterate: the aim in researching the consequences of employer-sponsored education is *not* to evaluate the success or failure of an individual literacy program or the usefulness of employer-sponsored education as a whole. Rather, I am interested in meanings and unacknowledged consequences. Thus I include qualitative as well as quantitative data in this chapter. Managers' comments about measurement will begin the discussion of consequences.

MANAGERS' PERCEPTIONS

The Measurement Problem

Interviewees were asked specific questions about the worth of the literacy education investment, their attempts to do a cost benefit analysis, the programs' impact on productivity, the existence of any formal or informal program evaluation practices, and their assessments of overall organizational effects. Many responded to these questions with comments about the difficulty of measuring organizational impacts and the problems of pricing education. Notably, nearly half of the managers were content with this lack of specificity, with such illustrative comments as the following:

> There are certain things that you really cannot put a cost on. We just recognized that it was another one of those areas that we as a company could do something to help our employees do their jobs better and feel better about themselves, so we just justified it on that basis. What is good is good, despite there being so much that is immeasurable. If it improves morale, and job performance, then let's do it.
>
> *Director of Personnel,*
> *Medium Sized Manufacturing Company*

> Management intuitively believes that education is working.
> *Director of Human Resources,*
> *Large Multinational Manufacturer*

> It enhances the company, and it is not measurable.
> *Human Resources Manager,*
> *Small Distribution Company*

Another responded that education was

> Like advertising, you never really know for sure what the
> benefits are.
>
> *Training Director,*
> *Small Community Hospital*

An equal number of managers, however, expressed frustration and a sense of inadequacy with regard to the difficulty of measuring results. Several hoped that gains could be quantified in the future. Their comments were succinct:

> This piece needs to be nailed down.
>
> *Manager of Training and Development,*
> *Large Teaching Hospital*

> Surveys have been taken, yet there are still no quantifiable
> outcomes.
>
> *Human Resource and Training Manager,*
> *Large Suburban Hospital*

> We have tried, but can't get good performance data on this.
>
> *Director of Human Resources,*
> *Large Multinational Manufacturer*

> We informally ask the supervisor, but there is not enough time
> to do more.
>
> *Workplace Education Director,*
> *Small Manufacturing Firm*

> We just don't have good metrics on this.
>
> *Education Specialist,*
> *Large Manufacturer*

Once they acknowledged that quantifiable outcomes were elusive, the managers interviewed were more than willing to recount *perceived* benefits—based on personal observation, anecdotal reports, or other "unscientific" means. In the discussion to follow, these benefits will be classified as either organizational or individual, even though it is conceptually difficult to distinguish the two since there are obvious areas of overlap. (For example, self-esteem improvements may help both the individual and the organization. And surely employees as well as firms benefit from safety improvements and job retention.) For purposes here, I have differentiated between direct organizational benefits and indirect benefits. The direct category includes items that are clearly organizational (though the argument can still be made that whatever benefits the company benefits the employee in the long term). The indirect category is my attempt to capture the overlap between individual and organizational. These organizational outcomes are noteworthy in the extent to which they do not reflect the managers' espoused motives for offering education, as well as in the fact that most are attitudinal.

Direct Organizational Outcomes

Viewed from a quantitative perspective, there are few commonalties in the list of direct organizational outcomes:

TABLE 2
DIRECT ORGANIZATIONAL OUTCOMES

Community approbation	2
Retention	2
Improved communication	2
Higher productivity	2
Cultural change	1
Safety improvement	1
Tax savings	1

A selection of quotations will elaborate upon these items. Two managers described positive public relations, referred to above as community approbation. One noted that employer-sponsored education was

> A good thing for the hospital to talk about, allowing them to be well respected in the community.
>
> *Employment Specialist,*
> *Community Teaching Hospital*

Another, from financial services, concurred, saying that

> People see that we are sincere about community reinvestment.
>
> *Assistant Vice President,*
> *Large Bank*

The productivity category included one manager who said "we get more out of the workers [because of literacy programs]." That productivity is not universally noted as an organizational outcome is a significant finding, given the rhetoric about the skill gap and competitiveness crisis that ostensibly motivated many of the managers. And it is surprising that communication is not more commonly cited, since language improvement was such a widespread goal (noted by nine).

Looking back to the list of managers' espoused motives, the following could be considered organizational (from Table 1: Competitive Pressures):

Customer	5
Retention	5
Safety	4
Quality	4
Regulation	2
Union	2

Nowhere on this list of motives is community approbation, though otherwise there are areas that overlap. The gap between espoused motives and reported outcomes gets larger as indirect outcomes are considered.

Indirect Organizational Outcomes: Attitude Changes

The "indirect" category primarily consists of attitudinal changes on the part of the worker, noteworthy especially because attitude was not a topic on the questionnaire. Managers were asked in an open-ended manner about outcomes, with no probes or suggestions. Many respondents (seventeen of twenty-five) mentioned such changes, and attitude was discussed in such a way that it appears to benefit the organization more so than the individual. According to the managers, the literacy classes positively affected learners' attitudes about work, about the organization, and about themselves. Table 3 summarizes these consequences; illustrative comments follow.

TABLE 3
INDIRECT ORGANIZATIONAL OUTCOMES

Loyalty	5
Participation	4
Confidence and self-esteem	4
Voice and initiative	3
Morale	1

They ask for special projects.

Manager of Human Resources,
Large Distribution Company

Success is measured in the enthusiasm.

Director of Personnel,
Medium Sized Manufacturing Company

[Managers don't much care] if curriculum is work related, because they also see such a change in the personality that indirectly it does affect their work, though they are not learning how to run a new dish machine or how to buff a floor, their presence in the hospital has become a much more positive presence.

Employment Specialist,
Community Teaching Hospital

In general we find positive feedback from the supervisors and we have better and happier employees.

Human Resources Assistant,
Nursing Home

Asking work-related questions was another commended attitude:

Anecdotal evidence showed that [their] managers valued the ability to speak up and reach out as key, not necessarily the language level. We have to figure out how to support this in terms of what we teach—adding assertiveness and perhaps more cultural awareness training.

Manager, Training and Development,
Large Teaching Hospital

The ability to say that "they don't know" represents that attitude we want here.

Assistant Vice President,
Large Bank

Finally, the employees' willingness to "do more" was bluntly noted by one:

They are not afraid to do more at work.

Education Specialist,
Large Manufacturer

As an outcome of literacy education, these attitudes are unanticipated if not surprising. The "educated" worker is enthusiastic about work, willing to "ask for special projects," and "not afraid to do more." Such attitudes affect job performance, though, to reiterate, these effects are not calculated or even greatly acknowledged. Employee attitudes towards their employer are also reportedly modified as a consequence of literacy classes.

Indirect Organizational Outcomes: Literacy and Loyalty

To expand upon the quote that was placed at the beginning of the chapter, a "positive view of the company" was a clear gain:

It took us about three months to find out that there were some
unanticipated dividends. [At the graduation ceremony], a student gave a wonderful speech of appreciation followed by others saying the same thing. Some of them who had been viewed
as having borderline attitudes were up there gushing with appreciation about the opportunities this company has given
them. So the unanticipated gain was in loyalty and positive
view of the company.

Human Resources Director,
Multi-National Manufacturer

At the end of the interview, managers were specifically asked whether loyalty
and commitment had increased. Twenty of them responded affirmatively. In
some cases the cause and effect were straightforward:

Absolutely more loyalty as a result, especially from ESL students. The advantage of doing it *onsite* is that employees feel a
greater sense of belonging, trust, and support.

Manager of Human Resources,
Large Distribution Company

On cultural diversity day, one employee stood up and said,
"This is the first company that ever encouraged me to learn
more." I see that as an example of loyalty.

Director of Inservice Training,
Nursing Home

Loyalty is an unanticipated consequence.

Human Resources Manager,
Small Distribution Company

Other managers were more aware of the tenuous causal relationship between
education and loyalty, but believed that it existed nonetheless. One described:

[The students are] smiling, talking, feeling better about themselves because of the programs. And they know it was funded
by us, that they tend to have greater loyalty.

Employment Specialist,
Community Teaching Hospital

It is important to note that loyalty and/or commitment were not universally
sought after. One manager commented that:

Greater commitment was not necessarily an outcome. Because
I feel that the contract has changed so much…that what people
really need to hear is that they have to take some personal responsibility for their individual development…but there are no
guarantees.

> *Human Resources Director,*
> *Medium Sized Manufacturing Company*[2]

Along the same lines, a different respondent hoped for
Loyalty to a career, not just a job. Higher commitment is a pro
and a con. We don't want stale employees.

> *Director of Training,*
> *Small Community Hospital*

Loyalty to an organization (or to a career) is an attitude change that could be
brought about by means other than literacy education. That literacy is considered
to be the vehicle is likely due to the value placed on education and the fact that
those at the lowest levels do not typically have access to such benefits.

Indirect Organizational Outcomes: Self-esteem

Many managers mentioned self-confidence and esteem as indirect results of employer-sponsored education. One said, directly:

Employees are more confident.

> *Director of Training and Organizational Development,*
> *Large Hospital*

When asked "why?" some reasoned that increased self-esteem was tied to language acquisition and English language ability, while others related it to specific
job-related skill improvements. Still others saw it as a reflection of the company's good faith effort to offer a valuable benefit. Others thought that low self-
esteem was tied to previous school failure, the sting of which was alleviated by
the forgiving environment of the workplace education classroom. By implication, managers believed that improvement in self-esteem would increase work
performance. Still, several were skeptical as to whether this was a good reason
for investing in education, one saying that,

Self-esteem alone is not enough. We need to focus on
productivity.

> *Director of Training and Organizational Development,*
> *Large Hospital*

In sum, literacy classes reportedly changed learners' attitudes about their work, their employers, and themselves. Managers highlighted these changes, perhaps as a substitute for evidence of productivity improvements or cognitive gains. Their attention to attitudes is all the more remarkable since attitudes were not mentioned as a motivation for beginning the workplace literacy program.

Learning and Change

Though not an explicitly noted outcome, several managers interviewed commented on the surprising demand for more learning that they observed in the participants in the literacy programs. One described a "cultural shift," saying,

> People carry their books around and discuss class-related things. I think we've laid the groundwork in terms of people knowing that there's more to learn and that it's interesting and helpful. I've seen a lot of change and noticed how supportive the group was of each other.
>
> *Human Resources Director,*
> *Mid-sized Manufacturing Company*

Success in the adult classroom can catalyze the employee to seek additional schooling, inside or outside the workplace. Some companies acknowledge the fact that employees will want more formal education—they use onsite basic education programs to offer a "jumpstart," and see their responsibility as getting the employee interested, getting them started in a classroom setting within the relatively safe walls of the company, and increasing their confidence that they can learn. Then employees are encouraged to complete their education outside the company. One respondent noted that ESL and ABE provided "a nice springboard to success," going on to emphasize how important it was for lower level classes to be graded only on a pass/fail basis so that the learners can have a positive experience and be motivated to go on to "a more competitive situation with grading," presumably in a community rather than workplace setting.

Inherent in the message about more education is the suggestion that employees should be open to workplace change. Two respondents spoke specifically of the importance of the learning *process* as being of greater importance than the product, because of the need for ongoing learning and change:

> Education is the epitome of change and openness—if you can do that in the classroom you can do it on the job and can better contend with the needs of the evolving organization.
>
> *Director of Training,*
> *Small Community Hospital*

> We believe that the literacy program will provide us with em-
> ployees that not only have better literacy skills but also are
> quicker at learning the new machines and are more involved.
> We did find that people who were in the program were better
> involved and more interested in influencing their environment
> rather than being influenced by it, and that was the kind of
> person that we wanted to see in the organization as we man-
> aged the change.
>
> *Director of Human Resources,*
> *Large Multinational Manufacturer*

The desire to learn more, be self-reliant, and accept change readily would be found in any description of the "educated person," so it appears that literacy programs provide education in the broadest sense, rather than narrow training. From the more pragmatic perspective of the work organization, these are sought after work attitudes, resulting in "the kind of person we wanted." Literacy education is both the springboard to more learning and the source of openness to change. Especially notable is that these attitudes are expected of those at the lowest organizational levels, whereas in the past such workers might be expected to passively take orders and complete tasks.

Assimilation and Diversity

The fact that so many students in workplace education programs are immigrants leads to another set of unanticipated consequences. Managers alluded to assimilation, appreciation of diversity, and the effects of classes on racial/ethnic tensions.

Assimilation occurs in a number of ways. First, since ESL classes are usually part of a menu of basic skills courses (including ABE, GED preparation, etc.) available to all employees, immigrants are not singled out as the only "educationally deficient group." Native and nonnative English speakers both leave work to attend class, so the experience is less isolating for the immigrants (though it may have the opposite effect on the native speakers in need of basic skills, since their deficiencies become obvious). Second, the ESL classes themselves often take as their subject matter the immigrant experience at work, primarily because adult education philosophy suggests classrooms that are participatory and reliant upon learners' experiences. Teachers ask students about national origins and native cultures as a way to create positive relationships and to design relevant lessons. By articulating the challenges of "Adapting to Life in the U.S.," as one curriculum module is entitled, the student can advance his or her own assimilation and integration. As well, the less than sanguine aspects of the assimilation process can be addressed through classroom materials such as the "Job Discrimination Curriculum." Third, integration and assimilation are realistically more possible as English capacity increases. When students become competent in the language and with their experience of adapting to the U.S., their self-esteem increases and they more confidently socialize and cooperate with the larger workforce.

Appreciation of diversity is a corollary consequence. One manager made the connection explicit,

> This literacy program says that we are respectful of diverse cultures.
>
> *Human Resource Manager,*
> *Mid-sized Retail Distribution Company*

Organizations that institute such programs cannot help but become aware of the diversity in their midst, since typically such basic skills programs begin with a needs assessment. One respondent said, "We had no idea how many nationalities were here until we surveyed them," and another stated, "I wish we could offer foreign language classes for our native speakers as well." Once the range of ethnicities and extent of difference are recognized, some companies further institutionalize diversity efforts. One of the firms added a soccer game to their annual picnic in order to accommodate the immigrant workers, workers who for the first time were able and willing to suggest such a change in tradition, ostensibly because of their literacy class experiences. Another respondent noted that "the [international] food was the best part of the graduation ceremony" and two other companies reported incorporating ethnic celebrations into their existing corporate traditions.

Several employers described being involved in "diversity programs," sometimes distinct from and sometimes in conjunction with their educational programs. A human resource manager reported adding a cross-cultural diversity class for managers as a result of having had the ESL/literacy class. It should be noted that in a few cases the educational strategy that motivated workplace literacy programs was being retooled as a diversity strategy. In one bank that had been forced to discontinue employer-sponsored education due to a merger and subsequent cost pressures, the manager interviewed said that she was hoping to reinstate the ESL classes "under the umbrella of the upcoming diversity initiative." This is not prevalent: most companies continue to view basic skills and diversity as two different issues, yet it may indicate a nascent trend.

It also appears that the workplace classes serve to diffuse potential identity-based conflicts. Several managers mentioned racial and ethnic tensions. For example, a frequently cited problem with workplace literacy is that often students leave their work assignments to attend class, and this causes resentment regardless of race or ethnicity. When the group is an easily identifiable minority, the resentment can intensify, and may take on racial overtones. One manager noted,

> With an increasingly Asian workforce leaving for class, racial
> flames can be fanned with peers and supervisors.
>
> *Manager of Human Resources,*
> *Large Distribution Company*

Group tension can exist in the classroom setting, where the teacher is expected to diffuse it. A human resources director reports:

> There was lots of competition—if not animosity—between
> Spanish and Portuguese workers. So that was a struggle for the
> teacher, and led to your basic management problems that re-
> sult from cultural differences.
>
> *Human Resource Director,*
> *Grocery Chain*

 Both of the incidents described just above would appear to heighten ethnic and racial tension, yet data suggest that the opposite happens. Because the class ex- ists, it serves as a safety valve. The teachers explicitly teach about cultural dif- ferences, as is the norm in the ESL curriculum, so the literacy class offers a place to address ethnic, racial, and even working class tension in the workplace. Aside from the obvious process by which this happens, that is, the teachers teach about difference and acknowledge the possibility for conflict, this happens in- visibly as well. The workers are grateful to the employer for offering literacy at work; moreover, immigrants need these jobs and the education, however mea- ger, so are unlikely to put either at risk.

Managers' observations about the consequences of workplace literacy reveal a range of organizational impacts, the great majority of which reflect changes in employee attitudes. Some of these attitudinal changes were directly articulated while others were inferred from comments about related program- matic topics. Overall, these impacts are impressionistic: measuring outcomes was an acknowledged difficulty. Nonetheless, these are consequential, and as interesting in their perceptions than in any proven reality.

ORGANIZATIONAL CONSEQUENCES: RESEARCHERS' FINDINGS

Other researchers had mixed findings when they tried to determine quantitative and qualitative benefits of workplace literacy programs to the or- ganization. Again, attitudinal changes dominate the discussion, though the measurement issue is not far behind. Three studies are of note:

1. Hollenbeck's large-scale statistical analysis devoted an entire chapter to impacts, saying, "Despite the importance of economic payoffs to both parties (employers and workers), almost nothing is known about them (i.e. the economic payoffs)" (1993:63). He offered anecdotal evidence of organizational impact, based upon data that he warned should be

considered "indicative rather than firm because it is simply *ex post* reporting of perceptions and there is no explicit counterfactual" (68). His eight categories of company outcomes are: retention, absenteeism/lateness, advancement/promotions, worker safety, output quality, customer satisfaction, scrap/error rates, and productivity. Of these, one area showed majority agreement that there had been a moderate amount of improvement, that of output quality. Customer satisfaction also improved according to a little over half of those surveyed. These were "far from overwhelming" results, to quote the author, especially when compared to improvements in basic skills and employee attitudes, where larger (though still only modest) gains were more consistently noted.

2. None of the seventy-two firms that Bassi (1992) studied attempted to quantitatively assess outcomes. Managers reported moderate to significant impact on the following areas, in more than half the cases: worker morale, communication ability, company loyalty, reading ability, quality of output, ability to use new technology. Again, these are not overwhelming, and the mix of attitudes and abilities is notable.

3. A 1999 report by the Conference Board (Bloom and Lafleur) asserted both "social and economic benefits," though not through bottom line assessment. Interview results showed that the highest percentage of respondents reported "improved morale/self-esteem" (87%), with three benefits tied at 82%: "improved quality of work," "better team performance," and "improved capacity to cope with change" (6). Like the managers cited above, and like the other research studies, this report highlighted attitudes and not quantifiable changes such as "quality," apparently trusting that positive economic benefits would follow.

These three reports confirmed the beliefs of the twenty-five managers with whom I spoke. Organizational outcomes can be identified, but they are not what might be expected given the rhetoric that surrounds literacy policy or the business writing concerning the need for workplace literacy. Firms ostensibly gain from changes in worker attitudes, though neither these gains nor the new attitudes are measured. I will show that these puzzling findings remain puzzling for several reasons, primary of which is to assure organizational cohesion. But first, the individual consequences of workplace literacy will be addressed.

INDIVIDUAL CONSEQUENCES

Managers' Perceptions

Managers described the consequences for employees, the majority of which could be described as positive. Several respondents noted negative outcomes along with the positive, and a few were unconcerned and/or unaware of any individual consequences. Outcomes were tabulated, and are clustered as material improvement, attitudinal changes, and educational gains:

TABLE 4
POSITIVE WORKER OUTCOMES

Material	14
Attitudinal	11
Educational	7

n=25 (some reporting several)

Material and attitudinal gains were the most frequent responses. Over half of the managers interviewed mentioned some kind of material gain for the workers as a consequence of the employer-sponsored education, with gain defined either as economic (pay or promotions) or as in the form of credentials (usually a GED or adult diploma). Of the eleven who described attitudinal changes, seven used the term "self-confidence," and three referred to a new-found willingness to speak. Specifically, respondents described "boldness," a worker who now "talks all the time, once class gave her permission," and the ability of some employees to speak to their children in English. These are differentiated from the attitudes cited in the previous discussion of organizational outcomes because they appear to offer benefit directly to the employee, rather than to the organization, though the distinction is nebulous.

Instructional gains were noted by seven, with most of the comments being about grade level improvements and language skills. Two managers declared that the individual educational gains were presumed but the details were not known to them, one citing privacy for the learner and professional responsibility of the adult educator for tracking student progress, another saying "class is class" and not tied to performance appraisal. This was a touchy issue—more than one program explicitly advertised confidentiality in order to entice the employee who might be afraid of coming to a basic skills course. Attendance is often a proxy for learning. Several respondents avoided specific outcomes by looking at the program as a whole and reasoning that the employees were experiencing positive benefits because attendance was good. One echoed this sentiment, saying, "they vote with their seats," implying that the students enthusiastically attended class and clamored for more, and that this was proof that the classes were accomplishing what they were intended to.

Finally, several managers avoided the issue of outcomes altogether or reported negative results. One stated,

> We leave all assessment of outcomes and curriculum decisions
> to our educational partner.
>
> *Human Resources Assistant,*
> *Nursing Home*

Another offered,

> Progress is slow in ESL—there are no overnight gains. Some
> are not literate in any language.
>
> *Manager of Training and Development,*
> *Large Teaching Hospital*

Another described a feeling of frustration on the part of the supervisor with the length of time that it took to see any results. Along the same lines, one manager expressed disappointment that

> So many still spoke Portuguese or Polish with their peers.
>
> *Director of Personnel,*
> *Mid-sized Manufacturing Company*

These negatives were all cited alongside positive gains, and the respondents endeavored to show that there was a range of consequences for individuals. In one case the negative reactions were attributed to the learning curve, that is, the manager felt that the organization had to do a better job preparing those who were involved for the fact that learning is not easy or quick or permanent. In another case, these negative consequences were part of the reason that the program was eventually discontinued.

What is remarkable is that managers did not calculate these individual consequences or track them in any systematic manner. Some, but not all, state-funded programs required evidence of individual learning along with proof that this learning resulted in occupational advancement, and labor unions also wanted assurances of pay increases for educational attainment. Even in these cases, the managers interviewed were largely unaware of the specifics, in part because they left such record keeping to the teachers, and also perhaps because as managers, they were ostensibly more concerned with organizational benefits, though these were also haphazardly calculated.

Other Researchers' Findings

Though the extent of individual gains could not be assessed in my interviews, other researchers have attempted to make a determination as to cumulative impact. Hollenbeck's review found a significant correlation between workers who participate in employer-sponsored education and increased earnings, though the author cautioned that there was no way to determine whether this was a causal relationship, since other variables that might affect earnings were not discounted (1993:73). He also noted attitudinal changes: "Another outcome occurs almost universally. These individuals cite improved self-confidence and self-esteem as a result of participating in these programs. Such payoffs are important to participants and lead them to continued participation" (82). Bassi discovered a similarly positive relationship between worker advancement and firms that had a workplace education program in place for two or more years (1992:37). Both of these researchers concluded that employer-sponsored education was more likely to be found in firms that were undergoing other work changes as well, explaining the difficulty of establishing causality. More recently, a meta-evaluation was conducted of the research on adult learning and literacy. (This was not limited to workplace programs, though workplace studies were included in the sample.) This study concluded that there were benefits for individuals who participated in classes: gains in employment, earnings, and self-image. Quite noteworthy, however, is the finding that literacy gains could not be documented by tests, even though learners themselves perceived that there had been improvements in reading, writing, and mathematics (Beder 1991:5). One interpretation of these findings is that adult learning cannot be measured by traditional methods; another perspective is to argue that perhaps there are only minimal literacy gains, but the appearance and perception of improvement is enough, particularly if material improvement is the primary goal.

So, overall, better earnings and occupational mobility appear to result from worker literacy programs, evident to managers and outside researchers. The causative mechanisms are unclear, however, due to the complexity of workplace dynamics. The unclear causation is made especially problematic by the paucity of attention to actual literacy gains. Learning improvements cannot be documented, but the individuals appear to improve their human capital. Again it appears that the symbolic nature of the literacy programs is at least as important as educative impact.

Consequences for individuals are broader than what has been discussed previously, since this section is specifically concerned with managers' articulations and the findings of other researchers. Additional analysis reveals that employability and a new contract are individual consequences of workplace education, addressed in the next chapter. Also considered separately will be the consequences for the middle managers themselves, an unanticipated finding yet one that ties together earlier arguments about the influence of external forces on the persistence of literacy programs.

UNINTENDED CONSEQUENCES: CONSENT AND COHESION

Literacy programs at work have observable impacts on organizations and individuals, in ways that are both predictable and surprising. Conclusions will be summarized, and further questions articulated:

- Managers do not closely scrutinize the results of workplace literacy programs, content to rely upon anecdotal data and their belief that education is good. *What are the unintended consequences of this lack of oversight?*
- At the same time, the organizational outcomes that managers do observe could have been achieved by means other than education, and there is no proof that the literacy programs had much to do with the results noted. *Why is literacy education the unquestioned mechanism?*

- The extensive discussion of attitudinal changes suggests that workplace literacy programs are lauded because they identify a "kind of person" desired by organizations, and these classes can engender organizationally desirable attitudes: loyalty, enthusiasm, openness to change, willingness to speak up. Improvements in self-esteem are especially notable. *What are the consequences of using literacy programs for such purposes?*

- None of the managers mentioned the desire for changes in work attitudes when asked about their rationales for instituting the literacy program. This gap between espoused motivation and observed outcome may be indicative of "latent functions,"[3] analysis of which will reveal the manner in which the programs contribute to organizational stability. *How does this gap contribute to the status quo? Are there other explanations?*

- Immigrants can be assimilated into organizations as a consequence of workplace literacy education, at the same time as such programs diffuse ethnic tensions and increase the acceptance of diversity. *Why are these consequences not more apparent in program justifications and evaluation studies?*

Inattention to Outcomes: Concealing Educational Deficiencies

At the most basic level, managers do not know how employees are progressing in their academic pursuits. Test scores are kept by teachers, and occasionally shared with managers, but the norm is to keep such achievement records separate from any work performance or reward considerations. The teachers rationalize this through concerns for student privacy and managers accept this explanation. Certificates of completion are granted, and occasionally a student will pass the exam for the GED or adult diploma. The fact that outcomes are not communicated (or measured in any organizational terms) has several possible explanations, embedded in ideology, the bottom line, and denial of the full extent of the literacy problem.

Even though skill improvement is only sketchily demonstrated, managers believe that educated employees are better workers. Discussion of institutional forces in the broader culture has established the belief in the education solution—everyone "knows" that education is beneficial. In this situation, it appears that the power of these ideological beliefs *diminishes* the managers' interest in careful scrutiny of outcomes, for both individuals and the organization. This may save the managers time and money, two pragmatic concerns, especially given the difficulty measuring impact.

At the same time, this lack of attention to outcomes may serve to divert attention from the true extent of the educational deficiencies of the workforce. The diversion can be understood as contributing to the stability of the firm, despite the legitimacy concerns engendered. The managers, understandably, hesitate to say, "we have X number of illiterate employees who have only managed to progress to the fifth grade level this year." Such acknowledgment would reflect badly on the managers and on the larger organization, whether hospital, bank, or assembly line. Therefore, if educational gains are not assessed, then true skill levels can be obscured, assuring continued belief in the soundness of managerial decisions. Perhaps the one manager who desired that the literacy programs be given *no* publicity unwittingly spoke for them all—employers don't assess outcomes because they don't want the knowledge made public. Such obfuscation benefits the organization, since continuing to employ illiterate employees seems to fly in the face of the expectation of organizational rationality and the desire for legitimacy—why keep employees who "only" function on a certain level, especially in light of all the rhetoric about the importance of human capital in the contemporary economy? So the inattention to outcomes works to say "we respect our people's privacy" on the surface, and underneath, "we don't really want to know their true literacy levels because it might reflect negatively on the organization."

An additional unintended consequence of the inattention to outcomes is that the organization's involvement in education can remain at a superficial level. If the impacts were measured and found to be inadequate, then the employer might be expected to devote more resources to literacy programs—truly transforming from workplace into schoolhouse. This would involve a significant amount of time and money, and is likely to be resisted by employers without significant public pressure. While the boundaries of responsibility may be blurring, they are not disappearing.

Symbolic Aspects of the Literacy Solution

Managers believe that literacy education results in a number of organizational and individual impacts, many of which could also have been achieved by alternate means. Yet the reliance on education is unquestioned. The institutional explanation is again valuable, but limited: yes, education is an all-purpose solution in U.S. culture, but why is it so useful to these organizations, given their current challenges? I suggest that literacy education may be the mechanism of choice because of the messages it imparts about educational deficits and the "kind of person" needed in contemporary workplaces. This is especially consequential given that so many students are immigrants. Furthermore, literacy symbolizes employer commitment to retaining existing employees, while at the same time sending the message that these workers are not to expect greater rewards. Employers can remain profitable, while at the same time appearing benevolent and legitimate. Thus the new schoolhouse thus creates consent to continued inequality.

By virtue of attending literacy class, students are reminded of their inevitable position in the firm structure and in the broader society, since their educational deficits must be openly acknowledged (even as the extent of these deficits remains clouded, as established above). Education is so highly valued that to be without basic literacy can stigmatize the learner, labeling him or her as a dropout or an outsider, deserving of his or her place. Thus workplace literacy affirms the polarization in U.S. society, even as it apparently improves material circumstances, however minimally. Literacy classes, like the traditional school-ing system, therefore assist in the reproduction of social inequities.[4] At the same time, the fact that literacy lessons are made available affirms the necessity of the organizational hierarchy. Even with an educational philosophy within the class-room that asserts equality and says "we are all learners here," the message is clear outside the classroom: there are some with knowledge and credentials and some without. Those without will continue to struggle, and will need superiors to direct their actions.

Not surprisingly, the literacy program participants usually remain the lowest paid individuals in the firm. The connection between these two facts is key: by appearing to improve skills, employer-sponsored literacy education al-lows the firm to continue to employ inexpensive labor. And by documenting that workers are lacking in basic skills, the firm can justify paying them at low lev-els. The logic is circular, and could be worded as follows:

> We cannot pay them more because they are illiterate; we want them to stay barely literate so that we will not have to pay them more. But we will sponsor a minimal workplace educa-tion program, with a broad curriculum, because this will result in more loyal employees with the desired work attitudes, and will signal to other constituents that we are acting responsibly in the face of changing work demands and increased competition.

This may explain why the programs continue: employers cannot afford truly literate workers, and really don't need them. So they offer education for its sym-bolic value, ensuring that only incremental improvement occurs. The appearance of skill enhancement and the legitimacy that accompanies such efforts allow the firm to remain profitable. The attention given to the literacy "crisis," constructed as such, diverts attention from other possible management incentives such as better wages. As a benefit, workplace literacy is relatively inexpensive when compared with health or dental insurance, or child care (or increased wages for that matter), thus allowing the employer to economically care for a valued seg-ment of its workforce. Yet such caring seems to be at the expense of more sub-stantial salary increases that would allow these workers to rise above the ranks of the working poor. Still, as a symbolic action, it buttresses the moral legiti-macy of the firm and of the capitalist system.

Finally, the realization that the employer limits the time allotted to learning suggests that true literacy is not the goal. To reiterate, class time and support to attend classes are constrained, and these educational efforts are so inadequate as to risk being ineffectual. Yet, however minimal, learners appreci-ate these efforts, and the fact that some employers pay students to attend class may send the message that literacy learning is a valued activity, as important as job tasks. Employees respond with loyalty, organizations with retention. In either case, the minimal time allocation sends students the message that they are not to learn "too much." At the same time, workplace education maintains students' hopes for a better future because such opportunities ostensibly level the playing field. So in this sense, employer-sponsored education functions to reinforce the status quo, and to situate responsibility for educational advancement in the individual rather than the system.

Literacy Education, Work Attitudes, and Consent

Another explanation for why there is so little attention to educational outcomes can be found in the suggestion that attitudinal outcomes are more important, even though managers cannot openly state so. As an unintended consequence of literacy programs, the low-level employees exhibit newly positive attitudes towards their jobs and their employer, having become the "kind of person" that employers ostensibly need. In the contemporary workplace, attitudes are thought to be more important than knowledge, particularly among low-skill, often immigrant workers.[5] Changed (i.e., improved) attitudes towards work are believed to result in more participation in decision-making, as well as other productivity enhancements, though the connection between attitude and behavior is not guaranteed (Perrow 1986:115). These attitudes are certainly positive from the employer's perspective, and might be understood as indicative of employee consent: loyal, happy, learning-focused workers appear to be in agreement with employers' goals. Consent is a subtle form of employer control, and the literacy program is a particularly ingenious way to bring about consent.[6] Other options are available for the employer who decides that changed attitudes are necessary: coercive mechanisms were used in the past, motivational seminars and rewards are among the activities that would be found in contemporary organizations. That the employer chooses to use basic skills education reflects the value that literacy holds, especially to those in need.

Literacy programs bring about attitudinal changes through aspects of the hidden curriculum.[7] In the learner-centered adult classroom, the teachers are less authority figures than facilitators, and respect for learners is fundamental. The ethos of participation pervades both curriculum and method, so the students get actively involved. Self-direction and participation combine to convey a tacit message of individual responsibility that contributes to self-esteem. This message may be well received by the learners, accustomed as they are to taking orders and not being asked their opinions. At the same time, there is an obvious overlap between the attitudes expected in the classroom and that of the transformed organization, whether it be the "high performance organization" or the "worker-centered workplace" (Stein 1989; Chisman 1992). In such places, workers actively participate in organizational decisions, and high levels of individual responsibility are expected.

Yet not all organizations have adopted this model, so the hidden curriculum may teach lessons in self-reliance and voice that are problematic for workers who face a traditional authoritarian structure and climate outside the classroom. There may then be a dissonance between the participatory ethos inside the classroom and the organizational norms outside of the classroom, where changed attitudes may not be appreciated. Still, even without organizational support, these implicit lessons may benefit the workers. Studies of children's schooling have shown that schoolwork that is self-directed can positively affect occupational attainment (Bidwell and Friedkin 1988), so it is plausible to hypothesize that workplace education, with its emphasis on independence and initiative rather than obedience and memorization, will result in greater individual advancement. Furthermore, research shows that high self-esteem is linked to greater mobility outside the firm (Noer 1993). This works against employers' retention goals, but may benefit the individual. Moreover, employees' inclination to find work elsewhere might be counteracted to a certain extent by the obligation and appreciation that the workers feel towards their employer.

It is therefore possible that employees get raises and promotions because of the attitudes that they learn through the hidden curriculum of the literacy classroom, rather than because of the overt curriculum that teaches cognitive skills. Along the same lines, the organization may experience productivity gains not because students can read or speak English better, but because they are more in tune with organizational goals, and their improved self-esteem inspires them to do a good job. Consent, rather than skills, is the mechanism by which the organization benefits. Using literacy programs to bring about these attitudes certainly benefits the organization, since the firm does not have to admit that consent is more important than skills. Such an admission would diminish legitimacy, and be considered politically incorrect in the contemporary social environment, where education is valued and overt control of workers is looked upon as old-fashioned, at best.

Employees' positive attitude towards learning produces another unintended consequence. Employees clamor for more classes, according to the managers interviewed, and workplace literacy provides a good springboard. However, by inspiring the employee to pursue additional education outside the workplace, employer-sponsored education reinforces the current location of adult education—that is, in the public sector. This also affirms the existing locus of responsibility for education—it belongs to the individual, who must seek it outside of work through traditional educational venues. Some employees do continue their education, but most cannot because they have other jobs, family responsibilities, or transportation limitations that make it difficult to access the external educational system. Nonetheless, the fact that the expectation exists has symbolic importance because it situates the responsibility with the employee, who then internalizes it. The company's responsibility is therefore limited—they may be the "schoolhouse" for adult learners, but the learners themselves are responsible for taking action. Also, responsibility is limited: workers who want to maximize their learning must do so outside the firm, in a traditional educational venue. Again, literacy contributes to the status quo while appearing to do otherwise.

Loose Coupling and Program Sustainability

The consequences of inattention to outcomes are exacerbated by the disparity between motives and outcomes. Employers espouse the rhetoric of competitiveness through workforce education, yet make little attempt to assure that the education either results in competitiveness or fulfills espoused organizational needs. I suggest that the disparity is useful to the organization in unarticulated ways, and is a typical characteristic of educational endeavors.

To recap the findings of Chapter 3, where employer rationales were described: employers were motivated to invest in employer-sponsored education for reasons of employee expertise, competitive pressures, and employee well-being. The preceding discussion, and Tables 2 and 3, indicates that the first and last of these sought-after consequences occur, that is, that as a consequence of employer-sponsored literacy education, employees are more skilled and happier. Yet further comparison of motives to outcomes shows little overlap. Especially notable is the gap between the motive characterized as "competitive pressures" and the paucity of outcomes to that effect. And only two respondents even mentioned productivity as an outcome, and though it was mentioned in the secondary research studied, it was not prominent. At the same time, as discussed in the previous section, attitudinal changes were routinely observed yet not mentioned when rationales were assessed. Thus there is a gap between motives and outcomes that needs to be explained.

The concept of loose coupling offers one explanation for such gaps in organizational behavior (Weick 1976). The argument is that the various components that constitute the phenomenon of "education" are not tightly connected; that is, parts are loosely coupled, and consequently, one part of the system can change without affecting the other. This concept of "loose coupling" extends from the macro level of the state to the micro level of individual learning outcomes. With regard to curriculum, the assertion is that curriculum topics are often loosely coupled with learning goals, and that learning goals are loosely coupled with individual learning outcomes. Taking into account the workplace literacy classroom, the concept of loose coupling illuminates the observed disjuncture between the rhetoric and reality. While managers and policy makers advocate competitiveness and a curriculum that is tailored to workplace needs, the participatory learning approach is as likely to prepare students for a drivers' license or to write a resume as to do their jobs more productively. The theory of loose coupling suggests that this is an inherent characteristic of the nature of the activity—education—rather than a result of this type of education in this particular setting. Loose coupling seems especially evident in the case at hand, due to the fact that most employer-sponsored literacy education efforts rely upon nonemployees to teach, and managerial oversight is minimal once programs are begun. So the gap between motives and outcomes can be explained by the fundamental organizational concept of loose coupling. Loose coupling helps educational programs persist, despite disparities between motive and outcome, and despite lack of attention to measurable benefits. This is true in the workplace and in the community setting because the models are so similar. The unintended consequence is simply that programs survive, without apparent substantiation.

Immigrants and the Status Quo

It is remarkable that assimilation is not more readily acknowledged in the policy rhetoric and management writing on the topic of workplace literacy, especially since assimilation was historically an explicit rationale for employer-sponsored education and foreign-born workers are an increasingly larger percentage of the U.S. labor force.[8] The contemporary rationalization for employer-sponsored literacy that emphasizes competitiveness and changing skills seems to overlook the fact that much of the "skills gap" may be a language/cultural understanding gap. This oversight of immigrants perhaps should not be surprising, given that the decade of the 1990s began with a backlash against immigrants and nonnative English speakers, as made apparent by California's Proposition 187, efforts to defund bilingual education in the public schools, and proposed tightening of immigration quotas. These sentiments are evident in the workplace, though not without repercussion: there has been a geometric increase in the number of cases filed with the Equal Employment Opportunity Commission (EEOC) by employees of firms that tried to institute an "English only" policy.[9] Anti-immigrant attitudes have been exacerbated by the fact of manufacturing jobs moving overseas as well as by the threat of formerly high-paid knowledge work going abroad, exemplified by computer programming being outsourced to Ireland and India.

The backlash has created a situation where companies can no longer openly boast of their immigrant workforce, while at the same time they must rely on this workforce even more so than in the past. The nonnative English speakers often have the positions within their workplaces that are most undesirable—in the hospitals, they are in housekeeping and the kitchen; in manufacturing firms, they are on the line or cleaning up; and in other service companies they work in the laundries or distribution departments. Not only are these the dirty and sometimes dangerous jobs, but also they are poorly paid and low status. Yet the immigrants are willing to do such jobs, and from the employer's perspective, they are good workers, better than the "Americans" who may have the basic skills but not the desired work attitudes. Some managers empathize with the experiences of these low status employees, one noting,

> These basic jobs need to be done and we need to show appreciation to employees for doing these jobs.
> *Human Resource and Training Manager,*
> *Large Suburban Hospital*

The implication is that it would be difficult to entice other—better educated, white, native speaking—people to do "these" jobs, the dirty work so often done by illiterate immigrants, racial minorities, or women.[10] Along the same lines, another manager spoke of "these" workers, saying "we need jobs for these people in our society." It appears that employer-sponsored education provides a type of reparation for the fact that the work is devalued and the system is unfair. Educational opportunity offers a modicum of restitution. ESL classes, under the rubric of "workforce literacy," allow employers to meet the needs of the immigrants yet not call undue attention to themselves for doing so.[11]

The sentiment goes two ways: the immigrants are grateful to have the jobs they have, and managers are thankful to have them. Furthermore, the employees appear appreciative of the opportunity to take classes at work, and the managers are grateful to be able to offer such a benefit. This is especially evident at graduation ceremonies, as numerous anecdotes were related in which the students publicly expressed their strong feelings of gratitude for their teachers, managers, and the company as a whole. That the immigrants are so grateful further strengthens the managers' commitment to supporting workplace education—managers come to view the classes as a way that the company can show their gratitude for the worker—something more than a benefit. As one manager said,

> The willingness of the company to invest in these classes should be seen as a great compliment to workers.
>
> *Director of Human Resources,*
> *Large Multi-national Manufacturer*

Companies do show appreciation, yet this appreciation does not take the form of pay or bonuses, but manifests itself as the intangible benefit of education, with its promise of social mobility and the American dream. By offering such a "promise," the equal opportunity myth can continue, and the status quo holds.

BELIEF AND ITS CONSEQUENCES: A SUMMARY

Although they did not measure either individual or organizational outcomes, these managers believed that the literacy programs were beneficial, albeit in unexpected ways. This conviction without substance turns out to be rather useful, for the firms and the broader society. A second important discovery is that attitudinal changes were the most frequently mentioned program outcome, though such changes were not explicitly desired. Analysis of other unacknowledged outcomes reveals that workplace literacy programs can be understood as having a range of effects: not only to increase skills and encourage consent, but also to assimilate immigrants, affirm organizational values regarding change, show employer beneficence, individualize responsibility for firm productivity, catalyze employees to more education, and obfuscate structural economic reasons for competitive success or failure.

At the same time, little of significance is changed by the literacy program. Taking into account immigrants as well as native speakers, it appears that workplace programs perpetuate the existing organizational reward structure by assuring that there are literate workers to perform less desirable jobs, workers who are grateful and loyal and inexpensive. Furthermore, these workers take on more responsibility even as they know their place—lessons learned from the hidden curriculum. While these are unanticipated consequences, they may not be unwelcome from the employers' perspective. These workers are hardly the symbolic analysts of the new economy; rather, they are the stalwart laborers, still essential and still undervalued. Literacy classes reify the meritocracy, at the same time as they ostensibly give workers the tools to climb the ladder. These so-called employability tools will be a subject of the next chapter, where the effect of literacy programs on the employment relationship will be explored.

NOTES

1. Despite ongoing efforts by training professionals to determine ROI (return on investment) even technical subjects and narrow training interventions are difficult to quantify. Yet quantifying the contributions of various human resource functions is an ongoing preoccupation of those in the field, both practitioners and scholars. For recent summaries of the research, see "HR's New Role: Creating Value (Interview)," *HR Focus* January 2000:1; and R. Owen Parker and Teri E. Brown, "People Practices and Shareholder Value," *Ivey Business Journal* 64, no.3 (January 2000):20. Measuring results of workplace programs is an emphasis on the government-sponsored "21st Century Skills Web Page,"< http://www.skillsnetwork.gov.>

2. These findings about the connection between loyalty and individual responsibility will be further addressed in the next chapter, where the individualized nature of the new employment contract is assessed.

3. Robert K. Merton developed the concepts of manifest and latent functions, and championed the usefulness of functional analysis as a way to understand social events. See *On Theoretical Sociology: Five Essays, Old and New* (New York: Free Press, 1967). Manifest functions are those that are intended and well known to participants. Latent functions are unintended and infrequently recognized by participants. It becomes the job of the sociologist to uncover the latent functions, to "debunk" (Berger 1963). Latent functions are important because they explain a portion of the seemingly irrational aspects of whatever social system is under scrutiny.

4. See Pierre Bourdieu and Jean-Claude Passeron, *Reproduction in Education, Society, and Culture,* translated by Richard Nice (Beverly Hills: Sage, 1977); and Samuel Bowles and Herbert Gintis, *Schooling in Capitalist America: Educational Reform and Contradictions in Economic Life* (New York: Basic Books, 1976). The final footnote in Chapter One describes their ideas on schooling and reproduction, and their theory of correspondence between the school system and the economic system.

5. The importance of attitude over actual skill level is the subject of revisionist thinking among labor and educational theorists. Skill improvement may not be enough, as Bassi notes: "A small but increasingly vocal band of observers of the workplace has begun to question whether education in and of itself, is the answer. [It appears to be] a necessary, but not sufficient condition for enhancing competitiveness" (1992:2). Competitiveness is enhanced through improved work attitudes and personal qualities, such as increased self-esteem, that are functional for the organization because they enhance productivity and control and minimize conflict. Doeringer asserted this quite per-

suasively, in a paper presented at the Academy of Management meetings entitled "The Future of Workplace Productivity Systems:"

> Raising foundation skills is a much-overrated solution to the kinds of productivity problems facing high-performance firms. The foundations of productivity that are valued by such firms are not those of knowledge and skills, but involve work force qualities such as flexibility, adaptability, teamwork, and problem-solving capacity. (1993: no page)

6. The process by which workers agree ("consent") to managerial controls is a controversial topic within the labor process control literature. The basic thesis is that the organization (at times through its culture [Kunda 1992]) establishes a pattern of normative or ideological controls, distinct from the labor process itself. Normative controls, known as hegemonic regimes, are contrasted with traditional coercive controls, as well as those considered bureaucratic and technological. Key theorists are Burawoy (1979), Howard (1985), and Edwards (1979). (See bibliography for complete citations.) The controversy surrounds the extent to which workers can simultaneously submit to consensual controls and exhibit oppositional consciousness. For an empirical assessment of this tug between consent and resistance, see Vallas (1993). Lincoln and Kalleberg (1990) also examine work attitudes and control, comparing the U.S. and Japan. And Vicki Smith (1990) analyzes the way in which employee involvement programs encourage consent while at the same time providing a means to resist difficult clients, offering slightly more control over conditions of labor. Sabel (1995) also suggests that new work practices give workers tools for appropriation and struggle, if not overt resistance.

7. In addition to the formal curriculum, defined as planned instructional activities, there are unspoken lessons in any classroom, through what is known as the hidden curriculum. The hidden curriculum has been described simply as "all the other things learned during schooling," so it extends beyond text and technique. Studies suggest that these tacit lessons take a variety of forms: how to satisfy the teacher's requirements, for example, or the range of acceptable sex role behavior. This broad definition is taken from J. Eggleston, *The Sociology of the School Curriculum* (London: Routledge & Kegan, 1977), 15. The seminal work on the hidden curriculum has been done by Philip W. Jackson, *Life in Classrooms* (New York: Holt, Rinehart, and Winston, 1968) and *The Moral Life of Schools* (San Francisco, CA: Jossey-Bass, 1993).

8. Nearly one in ten residents of the U.S. are foreign born, according to the Census Bureau in 1999, with the new arrivals most often coming from Latin America and Asia. During the years 1990-1998, the foreign-born population increased by 27.1%, nearly four times the 7.1% increase in the native population. The foreign-born share has been steadily increasing since its low point of 4.7% in 1970 (Blanton 1999).

9. For a summary of various cases, see Diane E. Lewis, "English-Only Policies Pit Workers' Rights Against Employers," *The Boston Globe,* July 2, 2000:H8. As for the numeric increase, she writes, "In 1998, for example, 91 cases involving such policies or rules were litigated in court by the federal Equal Employment Opportunity Commission, up from 30 in 1995. More than 240 cases were filed in September 1999."

10. Everett C. Hughes is credited with this formulation of "dirty work." In the essay "Work and the Self," reprinted in *On Work, Race, and the Sociological Imagination,* edited by Lewis Coser (Chicago: University of Chicago Press, 1994), he explains:

> Now every occupation is not one but several activities; some of them are the "dirty work" of that trade. It may be dirty in one of

several ways. It may be simply physically disgusting. It may be a
symbol of degradation, something that wounds one's dignity.
Finally, it may be dirty work in that it in some way goes counter to
the more heroic of our moral conceptions. (62)

He goes on to state, "Delegation of dirty work is also part of the process of occupational
mobility" (64), a factor that explains why women and minorities are typically found doing the undesirable, often degrading, tasks.

      11. Even the state seems unable to admit the extent of the needs of the immi-
grant workforce, as evidenced by the *Guidebook for Massachusetts Workplace Education
Initiative* (Boston: Massachusetts Executive Office of Economic Affairs, 1987) that expressed surprise at the focus on ESL.

6

"No Guarantees": Literacy, Responsibility, and Employability

Workplace literacy programs have wide-ranging consequences, for the employee and the employer. These consequences can be contradictory: workers better their material circumstances and self-esteem, without proven gains in literacy. Managers boast of improved worker attitudes, with minimal attention to productivity gains or cost benefit analyses. The boundary blurring that occurs with respect to responsibility is both real and negligible: work organizations are the new schoolhouses at a superficial level only because workplaces cannot devote the time and resources necessary to assure true cognitive gains. Consequently, literacy programs reproduce the status quo, while claiming to offer opportunity and advancement. Yet even as social and organizational stability is strengthened, other aspects of work organizations are changing, particularly the "contract" that encapsulates the relationship between employee and employer.

In this chapter, employer-sponsored literacy education is examined in light of what it reveals about changes in the employment relationship, the so-called new contract. In this new contract, there are "no guarantees," to quote the manager featured in the Gary Electronics case below. The employer has replaced job security with employability, ostensibly made possible by literacy education classes. The suggestion is that the paternalistic contract of the past is being replaced by one that is more egalitarian and partner-like.[1] This assertion of partnership will be interrogated at various levels throughout the chapter. I suggest, to the contrary, that an *individualized* contract is emerging, a contract that is unstable, inequitable, and isolating.[2] I will argue that increases in individual responsibility represent "peace of mind foregone"[3] to the employee, while at the same time it relieves the employer of prior obligations. I also show that the employability suggestion is paradoxical if not fundamentally misleading. Education plays a critical role in this new employment relationship, especially with regard to expectations of increased individual responsibility and the replacement of job security with opportunity for employability. Again, education is overvalued to the detriment of those without knowledge and skills, and employer rhetoric does not match the reality of the new contract. Because the contract exists in the context surrounding workplace literacy programs, the chapter will begin with an in-depth description of the changing employment relationship in one workplace.

CHANGING EXPECTATIONS: THE CASE OF GARY ELECTRONICS

That work organizations were changing was a given as this study progressed. The nature of the change and the implications for all levels of society had been debated in the academic literature and popular press for at least two decades.[4] This rhetoric about change often found its way into company attempts to justify their expenditures on literacy education, as established earlier. Managers were asked specifically if the literacy program was part of a larger restructuring effort, and nearly all responded affirmatively. The human resources director of a medium-sized manufacturing firm, known here as Gary Electronics,[5] offered an especially rich assessment, to be detailed below.

The literacy education program at Gary Electronics had been implemented in conjunction with numerous other changes, as the firm tried to reduce its reliance on defense contracts and keep up with changing technology. ESL classes had been available onsite for four years, and were explained as resulting from the company's commitment to employee self-development in the face of other organizational changes. When asked specifically about restructuring, this manager described the new requirements that the company had established for employees, and employees' reactions:

> People are being asked to take on a wider variety of tasks— formerly two things—now they need to do fifteen things. For some people, it really turns them on. They are bored at work and like having a larger picture. There is some real pride in ownership and in our team. For others, it is just crazy. It's like, "How dare you ask me to do all this work for no more money?" So it runs the gamut—it almost feels like people feel both of those things at the same time.... It's more exciting, but harder and more stressful and they have to think more.

Her comments show the shifting expectations that are at the heart of Gary Electronics' organizational restructuring efforts, and she describes the employees' ambivalence towards these changes. Those who resist "all that work and no more money" show that the employer's heightened expectations for effort and engagement are not fully reciprocated. More money is not likely to be forthcoming, however, because Gary Electronics, like others attempting to survive the "defense build-down" of the early 1990s, is experiencing financial constraint and is facing competitive pressures for the first time. This has resulted in expanded job tasks without more pay, and some workers feel that "it is just crazy," as the manager stated.

One way that the firm can attempt to mitigate the craziness is through the offer of literacy education. When asked to what extent education was considered part of their larger benefit package, the Gary Electronics manager answered "Yes—it's a big sell. We do use it in recruiting. Our brochure highlights tuition reimbursement and onsite training." When queried as to whether the company expected greater commitment from employees as a result of the education made available,[6] she responded (emphasis added):

> No, not necessarily. That's an interesting question. Because I almost feel that the *contract* has changed so much ... that what people really need to hear is that they need to take some *personal responsibility* for their individual development and that while they are here we'll do our best to find a way to use that, but there are *no guarantees*, even if there is no job here they have developed themselves so that they could go elsewhere. I'm not in the business of training people so they could then leave and get better jobs, but, I'm not sure that in my mind I'd tie it [employer-sponsored literacy education] to commitment.

This company does not want commitment in exchange for its offer of employer-sponsored literacy education. Rather it wants to make clear the changed expectations of the new contract. Instead of loyalty, Gary Electronics wants to encourage "personal responsibility." And, by implication, instead of better pay (referring to the first quote), the employer will offer education and "more exciting" jobs. Most important, Gary Electronics will offer "no guarantees" of future employment, thus violating one of the fundamental tenets of the traditional employment contract. The company has apparently substituted employability for job security—employability defined as the opportunity to "develop themselves so that they could go elsewhere."

Paternalistic attitudes are therefore replaced by expectations of responsibility and partnership. The Gary Electronics manager said, "we have started to see a cultural shift here." Along with personal responsibility, learning has become a valued element in the new contract. Education is taken seriously:

> We got a Portuguese group to come to ESL class. A year or so later, they arranged *on their own* to get a certification course [in a technical area related to the business]. This is very exciting, and of course human resources cooperated in whatever way we could. People carry their books around and discuss class-related things. I think we have laid the groundwork in terms of people knowing that there is more to learn.[7]

It appears that these employees have accepted the message about the contract having changed and have considered the pragmatic implications of "no guarantees." Once certified, this group of workers will be able to apply their newly acquired skills to their current jobs, and they will aiso have the formal credentials to seek employment elsewhere, should the time come when Gary Electronics can no longer employ them. On the surface, it appears that the workers are better off, even if they have no desire to go elsewhere, since the new employment conditions appear to be an improvement over the dead end jobs of the past. This seems to be a win-win situation: the employer gains more highly skilled workers who are taking "individual responsibility for their personal development" and are clearly able and willing to "think more" about their jobs; the workers gain tangible documentation that will enhance their employability "so that they could go elsewhere." The fact that the employer supports such specific training is not new, but the role that education plays in the enactment of the contract appears to be a recent phenomenon.

One additional point is worth noting. In the scenario described above, the group of employees effectively bypassed the human resources department and arranged their own training. This may not bode well for the training manager's continued employment at that company, since her role has been taken over by the newly empowered employees. In short, as a result of "pushing responsibility down," the middle manager has become dispensable. She may have taught them "too much."

The Gary Electronics case highlights a number of issues that arise from the examination of employer-sponsored literacy education in changing organizations. This firm is attempting to adapt to the turbulent economic environment through redesign of work and modification of worker expectations, and workers' reactions are mixed. There is tension between those who like the opportunity to become involved and feel pride in being part of the "team," while others want to be adequately compensated for their increased responsibility, and still others wish that their work had remained the same. As an organization in the process of transformation, growing pains were evident. The tension is heightened by the assertion that there are no guarantees of continued employment, yet there is the offer of onsite literacy. Education plays a key role in this changing contract here and elsewhere.

RENEGOTIATING PATERNALISM: INDIVIDUAL RESPONSIBILITY

Educational opportunity accompanies expectations of increased responsibility in changing organizations. When asked to describe the corporate culture, one manager described a time of flux, stating:

> The shift is more towards the individual taking responsibility for their own development and growth. The shift is towards managing down, pushing responsibility down. We [in the financial service industry] are coming into something that is maybe quite old in some areas: the team, TQM, trying to get out of the silo and the hierarchy and more into empowerment.
>
> *Human Resources Director,*
> *Multi-state Bank*

Among the many changes in this organization, the expectation that responsibility be "pushed down" is most relevant to the changing employment relationship. Individuals are expected to take responsibility for their own development, as well as for work tasks and decisions. This is the worker-centered workplace described earlier, also referred to as the individualized corporation.[8]

Responsibility and Literacy

Individual responsibility is made possible by improved skills and increased knowledge along with decentralized authority and changes to work tasks. Education becomes critical in this individualized corporation, since the individual worker does not always possess the skills and knowledge to take on the responsibility. Hence the importance of workplace literacy classes: the paternalistic relationship can be replaced by a move "into empowerment," provided that needed skills are taught. When discussing why his firm offered literacy at work, the training and development director of a multi-national manufacturer elaborated on this point:

> It's a partnership. We do our part, they do theirs. Companies don't take care of their employees anymore. People are becoming aware that they are totally responsible for themselves.

Companies no longer "take care," rather they offer opportunity for individuals themselves to gain rewards. As another manager asserted:

> Our goal is helping employees help themselves.
> *Training Director,*
> *Large Telecommunications Firm*

An apparent shift away from dependence and paternalism is evident—as one respondent noted,

I tell them, "do for yourselves, not just for us."
Manager of Training and Development,
Large Bank

So employees must help themselves, at the same time as they take greater responsibility for organizational decisions. Describing this as a partnership is appealing, in that adults are treated as adults, but partnership implies a degree of
equality that is not perceptible. These workers are still at the lowest tiers of their
organizations, with their bargaining power limited by their educational deficiencies and language barriers. By pushing responsibility down, employers appear to
benefit disproportionately, notwithstanding the partnership rhetoric.

Responsibility and Rewards

From the worker's perspective, more responsibility can have negative
ramifications. George Homans wrote explicitly about the consequences of responsibility in the workplace, "Pay is clearly a reward; responsibility may be
looked on, less clearly, as cost. It means constraint and worry—or peace of mind
foregone" (1958: 604). There is no doubt that many workers have experienced
"peace of mind foregone" due to ongoing economic turbulence, and the instability and individuality of the new contract no doubt exacerbate the "constraint and
worry." (Whether this has worsened in recent years is an empirical question, not
addressed here. For illiterate workers at the bottom of the organizational hierarchy, it is likely that even the old contract held its share of constraint and worry.)
In the contemporary environment, individual responsibility can be understood as
a cost rather than a reward for the worker. Real rewards, in the form of money,
advancement, job security, or other material benefits, would be a less ambiguous
response to changing employment conditions.

Financial fairness seems a prerequisite for an employment relationship
based on partnership or mutuality. That this has not happened is a significant
challenge to the current rhetoric. As employees become responsible for work
formerly done by their superiors, the employment relationship appears to have
become not only individualized, but also inequitable and unfair, since increased
responsibility is not directly accompanied by increased rewards. Without more
equitable compensation, the employment relationship cannot be a partnership,
and the new contract appears to lack even the paternalistic protections of the old.
The language of partnership and mutual benefit is belied by the reality of an
employment relationship premised upon individual responsibility without individual power.

Conflicting Responsibilities

Even beyond the reward issue, individual responsibility may be seen as
a negative (or confusing) development with regard to literacy attainment. The
expectation of individual responsibility results in conflicting demands on the

employee, demands that can negatively affect educational attainment, as in this example:

> Classes during work time can create stress in terms of coverage—supervisors can cover, but what actually happens is that the learner decides not to go to class—this is a big challenge for us in training.
>
> *Training and Education Director,*
> *Large Hospital*

If the learner is expected to decide whether or not to go to class, then it is entirely likely that the learner may not attend class, if doing so will inconvenience peers, supervisors, or customers. (Complicating this decision is the potential for racial and ethnic tension, due to the large immigrant presence.) By encouraging the employee to consent to making the organization's goals her own, and consequently to stay and provide coverage rather than go to class, the burden associated with individual responsibility is made obvious, as is the clash between rhetoric and true opportunity.

Employees are not helpless in the face of increased and occasionally unrealistic demands. Even as enthusiasm is evident, worker resistance in the literacy classes has also been observed (Gowen 1992). As one manager stated, "You can't make them learn." The managers are directly affected by such challenges to their authority, which is the subject of the next chapter. For purposes here it should be noted that "pushing responsibility down" is a risky undertaking for the organization as well as the employee, since employees may not be willing or able to do what is asked of them. However, even this has unanticipated benefits for the organization as a whole.

Individual Responsibility and Firm Success

Responsibility that has been "pushed down" situates the success or failure of the firm in its employees (workers and managers) and their learning, thereby lessening senior management's responsibility for strategic errors, and diminishing the importance of the structural shifts in the world economy that likely have made competitiveness more of a challenge. By shifting this burden to the employees, the employers can essentially blame the victims if the strategy fails and the firm must close or layoff workers.[9] Clearly the stakes are high. By locating the problem and the solution in employee education, workplace literacy individualizes the employment relationship and effectively individualizes the success and failure of the firm, keeping attention away from the structural forces affecting organizational success. Thus the education solution, by enabling individual responsibility, becomes even more highly valued. This value extends to the cornerstone of the employment relationship, job security.

ILLITERACY AND INSECURITY

Several decades of layoffs in all types of industries suggest that secure employment is elusive in the contemporary economic climate. However, as established in earlier chapters, employers continue to value existing employees, and retention is one of the explicit motives for offering a workplace literacy program. Yet retention has become contingent upon employees' willingness to change, often operationalized as willingness to attend literacy classes. The following quotes illustrate these sentiments:

> We try to give them every opportunity—we don't want them to leave.
>
> > *Training Director,*
> > *Small Hospital*

> We have long-term employees, who have been very faithful and loyal to the company, and we felt some obligation to at least give them some opportunity to retrain and retool before we just went through with an ax and hired more literate employees.
>
> > *Human Resources Director,*
> > *Multi-national Manufacturer*

These quotes indicate that in the eyes of the managers educational opportunities are linked to continued employment; implicit is the use of job insecurity, rather than job security, as a motivator.

Negative Motivation

In this climate of insecurity, illiteracy as well as literacy programs can be threatening to low-level workers. Literacy programs call attention to employees' lack of education in ways that were less visible before employer-sponsored education was made available. Several managers described the fear that employees had that they would lose their jobs if their illiteracy were known, a fear that resulted in refusal to come to class or take a needs assessment test. In one firm, there was such strong resistance to having reading levels tested at the beginning of the literacy program that a legal ruling was sought to determine if refusal to participate in the assessment was grounds for dismissal. (It was, according to their in-house counsel.)

Employers use illiteracy and insecurity to create new workplace norms. When asked whether employees were given pay increases after completing ESL classes, one respondent answered "No," going on to state:

> In fact there is a vague negative motivation that we've tried to soft sell. The idea is that that's what's required today. And at some point it's going to become an issue if we can't close the

gap on these skills. If somebody were to say "hey, I'm not interested in learning English and I'm not interested in any stu-
pid classes," then there would be a negative consequence, because we can't really tolerate that.

Human Resources Director,
Large Medical Manufacturer

The "vague negative motivation" was alluded to by others. Several interviewees
reported an increase in interest and enrollments whenever there were layoffs or
rumors of restructuring.

We get lots more calls if there are rumors about downsizing.

Training and Development Director,
Multi-state Bank

We see more faces after a layoff.

Training Manager,
Multi-national Telecommunications Firm

These managers report that workers believe that educational upgrading will assist them in maintaining their employment in their current firm, or in developing
adequate employability to get a job elsewhere.

Under the old contract, illiterate employees could rely upon continued
employment as long as skill requirements remained stable. In the newly emerging contract, neither stable work requirements nor continued employment are
part of the bargain—literacy and ever-higher level skills are "required," ostensibly by forces beyond the control of the employer. Since the new knowledge/skill
expectations are ill-defined (e.g., no one can say how much English proficiency
is 'needed,' and the minimum math skills are continually under debate) the result is uncertainty and contract instability for both the employee and the employer. Workplace education becomes a tangible manifestation of the insecurity
faced by current employees, as much as it is an opportunity, benefit, and
incentive.

Offering Employability Instead

Given this uncertainty, the offer of employability was regarded as
beneficial by the managers with whom I spoke. Several suggested that the educational opportunity being offered is for the employees' future well-being as
much as for the organizations' benefit in the immediate present. Referring to the
long quote about Gary Electronics that opened this chapter, the statement was
made that "even if there is no job here, they have developed themselves so that
they could go elsewhere." Other managers affirmed this sentiment:

English classes would increase their marketability.
Manager of Human Resources,
Medium-sized Retail Distribution Center

Even if they don't have a job here, we have helped them prepare for their future.
Training Manager,
Teaching Hospital

Also, employees appeared enthusiastic about these opportunities to "prepare for their future." Managers were surprised at how willing the workers were to go to class, and commented upon their enthusiasm, gratitude, and interest in continuing their education. To quote from several:

We have lots of repeats. They will stay and try new courses.
Training Manager,
Multi-national Manufacturing Firm

All are so eager to learn.
Training and Development Director,
Multi-state Bank

I learned that even older adults want to keep on learning. And it takes so little to get them going, then they take off.
Human Resources Director,
Large Hospital

We had full attendance—they even wanted to bring their friends.
Training Director,
Small Hospital

Notwithstanding vague negative motivations and uncertain future work skill requirements, managers and workers are by and large enthusiastic about these classes and the future opportunities they promise. However, like individual responsibility, employability deserves careful scrutiny. Even though workers and managers are willing to go along with the idea, there is potential for further "peace of mind foregone."

EMPLOYABILITY AND INSECURITY

Employability is flawed, both in theory and in practice. First, I suggest that the employability argument is paradoxical at its core, since employers espousing this rhetoric are tacitly admitting that they may not need educated workers, but that some elusive *other* employer will certainly be eager to hire them especially if they are skilled and credentialed, or at least literate.[10] The further implication is that the current employer either has little faith in the firm's long-term viability or believes that future success will only be possible if existing lower level workers are laid off, the layoff being more palatable to all involved if the employer has helped increase the workers' human capital by offering education. Not only is this paradoxical, it is deeply unsettling for contemporary employees. The fundamental employment relationship is shaken by this realization of its tenuousness. Given the loss of trust in a particular employer, workers and managers must place their faith in the larger economic system, a system fraught with uncertainty due to blurred boundaries and shifting responsibilities.

A second flaw in the employability argument concerns the existence of adequate numbers of "good" jobs in this larger system. The assumption is that there are enough jobs that pay a living wage, but there are not enough workers with the requisite skills. The data about numbers of jobs at what level are confusing, as the previous discussion of overreaction revealed, though the argument has been made that "there are simply not enough decent jobs for the number of people who need them, not matter how well trained they are" (Lafer 1994:350).

So employability, even in theory, seems an irrational proposition, certainly an inadequate substitute for employment security. Finally, in practice, literacy programs as currently construed cannot offer much in the way of employability. In part, this is because credentials and diplomas have become so necessary.

Credentials and the New Contract

As a tool for advancement, the concept of employability rests upon credentials as much as real knowledge (Brown 1995). This is problematic when the subject is literacy, given the nature of basic skills learning and the limits that employers have instituted. While all participants may (or may not) have gained in their prose, document, or quantitative capacities, these gains are difficult to translate into employability outside the firm without an accompanying credential. Certificates of achievement are typically granted to "graduates" of workplace education classes, but it is a big leap from a teacher-created ESL certificate to the widely recognized credential of the high school diploma. Yet it is the diploma that will substantiate their achievement and certify their employability.

Diplomas are difficult for adults to obtain, particularly in a workplace-based program. Part of the problem is the limited time and support given to learning, as established in earlier chapters. Furthermore, only a few employers interviewed included GED or adult diploma classes in their onsite offerings. Among those that did, there were enthusiastically recounted anecdotes of the one or two workers who "went all the way" to the diploma stage of achievement. These few were clearly the exception, yet they were lionized by the training managers in order to illustrate the possibility of individual achievement within the workplace context. Therefore one of the fallacies of the new contract is exposed—because legitimate credentials are so difficult for those at the bottom to attain, employability is more a promise than a reality.

It must also be noted that the importance of a high school diploma has diminished in the past several decades. In this economy, the college degree is increasingly seen to be the minimum requirement to attain a "good" job. Katherine Dudley writes in *The End of the Line*, her ethnography of a plant closing,

> Today autoworkers know they cannot simply walk away from the credentialist standards that are applied to everyone in this society. At some level they too accept the idea that college degrees are "badges of ability." At some level we are all like the Scarecrow in the *Wizard of Oz*, believing that without the diploma we have no brains. (1994:181)

Employers often offer tuition reimbursement for college degrees, but those without fundamental literacy skills find it especially difficult to get to the point where they can take advantage of that benefit.

At the same time, there is growing recognition of the fact that credentials may *not* be "badges of ability." Recall the public school failure rhetoric, and the employers' lament that students can graduate from high school and still lack basic skills.[11] So the diploma is not the sure route to employment that it may have once been. It is possible, as well, that cognitive skills are less in demand than "soft skills"—the work attitudes deemed necessary for the high performance workplace (Capelli 1995). Yet such skills are difficult if not impossible to certify, even as they may be a crucial component of employability.[12] Where does this leave the barely literate worker? With little recourse but to attend classes and seek certifications. At present, high school and college degrees have no acceptable substitute in the broader labor market, and the workers most in need of such credentials are in no position to challenge their influence.

The counter-argument, at the heart of the individualized new contract, is the belief that workers *could* attain credentials if only they tried hard enough. Thus the employees can be held responsible for shortchanging their own future opportunities if they do not take advantage of the education being offered. By placing this responsibility on the learner/worker, the employer is relieved of prior commitment, and the individual is then blamed for not investing in the skills needed to assure continued employment. At the same time, the fact that employees are so enthusiastic about attending classes yet don't necessarily progress all that far might be understood as an illustration of the "cooling out" phenomenon (Clark 1961). Literacy classes allow employees to feel that their firms are assisting them to navigate the newly turbulent and demanding environment, yet the needed credentials are so difficult to attain that the student may decide that he or she is incapable. Students then drop out, or lower their aims, content with their limited achievements and low status and without the knowledge and confidence to make further demands on the firm, or the system as a whole. Their ambition is cooled out, yet they internalize the responsibility for such, adding to the idea that the contract is individualized and the employment relationship is all the more insecure.

EMPLOYER-SPONSORED EDUCATION AND THE INDIVIDUALIZED CONTRACT

Whereas in the old contract the employer offered a degree of job security, in the new contract, this offer is withdrawn and replaced with education, an opportunity that must be pursued by the employee, individually. This is like taking away a blanket and giving someone knitting needles, or using the biblical metaphor, teaching them to fish; the nature of the exchange is fundamentally altered. While in the long run such a change may well result in an empowered independent employee/partner, until other aspects of the relationship are transformed and until the education offered is more than superficial, the rosy rhetoric surrounding the "individual opportunities" of the new contract should be viewed with skepticism, as should the ostensible fairness of the offer of employability. This is a world of "no guarantees."

Workers in search of jobs and security—and employability—are most harmed by these practices. This is not to suggest that education is not beneficial, but rather to reiterate that alone it cannot deliver the jobs, wages, and productivity that are needed for individual and organizational success; and furthermore, it puts undue focus on the individuals rather than on the employing organization or the economy as a whole. Essentially, employers are able to rationalize continued inequities, limiting employability while appearing to do the opposite.

Structural economic changes, not illiterate workers, have caused recent shifts in the competitive environment, and, while it may be true that no single organization can be held responsible, in "pushing responsibility down," the company is creating an impossible situation, one that literacy classes will not alleviate. Such unrealistic expectations result in a fundamentally inequitable and unstable employment relationship, despite the talk of mutual benefit and empowerment. The new contract in the new schoolhouse works to further disadvantage the low-level employee, while it purports to do the opposite. The next chapter will turn the focus to the middle managers that have been charged with the implementation of this individualized employment relationship. Literacy education has a set of surprising consequences for this group, analysis of which will add to understanding why such programs persist and who benefits.

NOTES

1. The literature on the new contract spans a range of academic disciplines. Organizational psychologist Denise M. Rousseau provides an empirical and theoretical overview in *Psychological Contracts in Organizations* (Thousand Oaks: Sage, 1995). The idea that the new model is one of partnership is developed by political scientists Kenneth Chilton and Murray Weidenbaum in *A New Social Contract for the American Workplace: From Paternalism to Partnering* (St. Louis Center for the Study of American

Business, Policy Study Number 123, 1994). The sociological perspective suggests that changes in the contract cannot be assessed apart from other changes in the work organization and the economy as a whole. An example of this perspective is provided by Arne L. Kalleberg and Torger Reve, "Contracts and Commitment: Economic and Sociological Perspectives on Employment Relations," *Human Relations* 45, no. 9 (1992): 1103-1132. Sociologists Chris Tilly and Charles Tilly in *Work Under Capitalism* (Boulder, CO: Westview Press, 1998), take a highly structural approach to understanding changes in contemporary work arrangements, and suggest the possibility that the employment contract has become individualized. For an illustrative, and surprisingly critical, example from the management literature, see Barbara Ettore, "Empty Promises: The New Employment Contract," *Management Review* 7, no. 85 (1996):16.

2. Manuel Castells, in *The Rise of the Network Society* (Oxford: Blackwell, 1996), uses the idea of the "individualization of work" as he describes individual traits and flexible work arrangements as becoming more important. Michael Indergaard builds upon this to suggest that individualization is made possible through the network of employment brokers, that is, retrainers. See "Retrainers as Labor Market Brokers: Constructing Networks and Narratives in the Detroit Area," *Social Problems* 46 (February 1999): 67-84. I suggest that internal mechanisms such as employer-sponsored education and training also contribute to the process of individualization.

3. George Homans used this phrase in his classic article on exchange theory, "Social Behavior as Exchange," *The American Journal of Sociology* (1958): 597-606. Generations later, his attention to the potential inequities of exchange in the workplace is still relevant, notwithstanding assertions that the new exchange is partner-like. Peter Blau's work on exchange is also still influential. See *Exchange and Power in Social Life* (New York: Wiley, 1964). Especially useful is Blau's typology of exchange value, which allows the equity of the exchange to be questioned. In this typology, literacy education has *universal* value, as opposed to the *particularistic* value of job security.

4. Many consider this debate to have begun with Daniel Bell's *Coming of the Post-Industrial Society* (New York: Basic Books, 1973). Tilly and Tilly (1998) provided a thorough update, theoretically and empirically provocative. More directly pertinent to the issue at hand, Bassi (1994) found a strong correlation between transformation to a high performance or worker-centered organization and implementation of a workplace literacy program, and made this the core argument of her monograph *Smart Workers, Smart Work* (1992). A critical "sociocultural" analysis of management rhetoric surrounding the economic changes is found in *The New Work Order: Behind the Language of the New Capitalism*, by James Paul Gee, Glynda Hull, and Colin Lankshear (Boulder, CO: Westview Press, 1996). In Chapter 3, "Alignments: Education and the New Capitalism," they essentially update Bowles and Gintis (1976) for the postmodern world and its " fast capitalism."

5. "Gary Electronics" was selected as a representative case primarily because the manager was insightful and loquacious, a classic key informant. It is also true that the organizational and competitive changes she described were not unique (see citations just above), although, as a technology firm, Gary might have been slightly ahead of the curve with regard to work reorganization and technical training. Her suggestion that "the contract has changed so much" was a serendipitous finding that altered the remainder of my interviews and the course of my analysis.

6. The idea that literacy education could lead to increased organizational commitment is my own, though the corporate use of such benefits is a core tenet of welfare capitalism. The link between other employee benefits and commitment is explored in James R. Lincoln and Arne J. Kalleberg's *Culture, Control and Commitment* (New York: Cambridge University Press, 1990). For a noncritical assessment of the connection between commitment and management control, see the article by Richard E. Walton, "From Control to Commitment in the Workplace," *Harvard Business Review* (March-April 1985): 77-84.

7. Parts of this quote were used in earlier chapters, but it has been repeated here in its entirety because it adds necessary context to the new contract discussion.

8. See Sumantra Ghoshal and Christopher A. Bartlett, *The Individualized Corporation* (New York: Harper Business, 1997). These authors devote an entire chapter to a new moral contract, "a fundamental change in management philosophy." They state,

> In this new contract, each employee takes responsibility for his or her "best in class" performance and undertakes to engage in the continuous process of learning that is necessary to support such performance and constant change. In exchange, the company undertakes to ensure not the dependence of employment security but the freedom of each individual's employability. (284-285)

9. Congruent with William Ryan's understanding of the phrase, such attention to individuals as the source of problems and solutions serves to divert attention from structural analyses. See *Blaming the Victim* (New York: Vintage, 1976).

10. The evidence of declining internal labor markets appears to bear out this unspoken acknowledgment. See Tilly and Tilly (1998) and Harrison (1998). Harrison also asserts that payoffs to seniority are also shrinking over time, both across the workforce and over the careers of specific individuals. See Figure 2.3, page 19.

11. This is a controversial topic. The 1999 Conference Board report, *Turning Skills into Profit* by Michael R. Bloom and Brenda Lafleur, extensively documented the limited skills of diploma holders, asserting that "Even college graduates suffer from the skills gap: 16 percent have inadequate basic skills" (3). At the same time, it is important to recall the overeducation argument set forth in Chapter One, along with the critique of the future work skills literature (FWSL). Moreover, Bowles and Gintes (1976) suggested that "credentialism" is a critical arena for discrimination, and the Japanese have gone so far as to coin a term that translates as "diploma disease." See Ronald Philip Dore, *The Diploma Disease: Education, Qualification, and Development* (Berkeley: University of California Press, 1976).

12. Employers can screen for these types of skills through the pre-employment interview, where racist attitudes are believed to be made manifest. See Phillip Moss and Chris Tilly, " 'Soft' Skills and Race: An Investigation of Black Men's Employment Problems," *Work and Occupations* 23 (1996): 252-276.

7

Managers, Power, and Education:
Contradictions of Location

Thus far this book has documented the effects of workplace literacy on illiterate employees, its impact on sponsoring organizations, and its influence on the employment contract. While middle managers have been the sources for much of this knowledge, they have not thus far been the subjects of analysis. Yet, one of the unexpected outcomes of this study was the effect of the literacy education programs on the managers themselves, and the extent to which the managers use these programs to accomplish their own ends.

In this chapter, managers' voices will reveal the tensions and satisfactions they experience as they negotiate their location in the middle. Managers are key actors as literacy programs unfold, even as learners are the most obvious recipients and teachers have a great deal of autonomy regarding the content of the learning. The managers create the conditions under which the programs operate, and are invested in the symbolic and actual outcomes. As stated earlier, a great deal is expected of workplace literacy, and these managers are the organizational actors who are expected to accomplish it all. Yet these middle managers must answer to the senior executives above them, whose expectations are often unrealistic. Workplace literacy programs allow managers a place for resisting corporate demands. By insisting that the programs are needed, and by obfuscating the true nature of the outcomes and the problem, the managers assert their power versus senior management's expectations of easy solutions and flattened organizations. From this perspective, the middle managers are both agents and subjects of organizational change, literally caught in the middle.

MANAGING FROM THE MIDDLE

Within the new schoolhouse, the managers responsible for training and human resources find that their terrain has become contested. This is not the contest over privatization anticipated by critics of employer-sponsored adult education, nor is it a contest about corporate control of educational curriculum, suggested by social theorists. Rather, it is a personal challenge, concerning managerial authority and the meaning of managerial work. These managers have authority because of their place in the organizational hierarchy, but this power is circumscribed by the dictates of those above them and challenged by educated and empowered employees from below. Additionally, their position in the middle is threatened as organizations flatten.[1] Middle managers cannot help but worry that their continued employment is in jeopardy. Therefore these managers must continually reassert their contributions to organizational success, while at the same time they mitigate their employees' anxieties and keep senior management satisfied by managing in the "corporate interest."[2]

Managerial control is therefore less certain, though no less important. In this continual negotiation, such programs as workplace literacy create a new arena for power and control. Control of educational opportunity is imperfect and perhaps fundamentally flawed, yet this is little acknowledged in the managerial belief system.

The managers interviewed for this project were responsible for the day-to-day operation of the literacy education programs, and were often the primary program spokespersons and advocates. Whether they all should be referred to as middle managers is debatable; some might more accurately be labeled human resources or training specialists, and may not have any employees reporting directly to them. For purposes here, respondents as a group will be considered as being in the middle, since they share the essential qualities of being responsible for the literacy programs, and are located neither at the bottom nor at the top of the organizational hierarchy. As managers, they are considered agents of the employer; that is, they are expected to act in ways that bring about organizational, rather than individual, goals. Still, as their comments will reveal, they are not passively responding to their employers' expectations, but are actively creating the conditions under which these literacy programs can meet multiple needs. The middle managers use their autonomy and their managerial discretion in ways that benefit not only the organization, but also the workers and themselves.

The managers do a great deal of work that is typically considered managerial: they act as boundary spanners, constructors of meaning, and gate keepers in the context of implementing literacy programs. Each of these roles serves to affirm the continued necessity for their own position by increasing their power within the organization; and each role allows for maintenance of control over their own labor processes as well as those below them. Inevitably, too, the managers face conflict in this process of juggling multiple constituencies, as will be evident in the discussions that follow.

Constructing Meaning

Middle managers, along with senior executives in some cases, are responsible for explaining employer-sponsored literacy education to organizational and community members. They must create a logical rationale for why they institute such programs, and why programs should persist. In some cases they go so far as to construct (and reconstruct) the definition of literacy. One manager spoke about her desire to "raise the bar" once people finished the basic skills classes, by "offering courses in conflict resolution, quality, and teams," thus assuring her continued employment and sustained superior position despite newly literate workers. In another example, a respondent cheerfully acknowledged his plans to change his company's definition of literacy, saying:

> Once we get everyone above a standard, however, my challenge will be to redefine what literacy is and how you prove that. Or we may focus on another part of the organization.
>
> *Human Resource Director,*
> *Multi-national Manufacturer*

By constructing meaning that reflects their own knowledge of the "needs" of the organization for particular skills, along with the educational "needs" of the illiterate employees, program managers can assure their continued employment by implicit justification of intermediary positions such as theirs. Managers attain legitimacy for their roles, as well as for their programs.

Managers visibly construct the meanings accorded to the literacy programs in a number of additional ways: they write proposals for internal budget approval and external funders, speak at conferences on literacy and workforce development, create brochures to recruit new students and alert supervisors to the programs, and describe employer-sponsored literacy education for annual reports and other public relations outlets. One brochure, written for students and supervisors but made available to organizational outsiders, typifies the positive message:

> The Department of Education and Training, a division of Human Resources, is dedicated to helping [this company's] employees advance in their personal and professional lives. Each year, through hundreds of course offerings, we make it possible for thousands of employees to acquire new knowledge, sharpen job skills, and improve performance and productivity. Subject areas for individual skill development include reading, writing, math, English as a Second Language, and preparation for the high school equivalency exam (GED). In addition to providing practical training that meets

individual needs, these courses can help lay the foundation for further
career development.

Since education is so culturally valued, casting literacy in a positive light is not
especially difficult. Individual benefits are highlighted, rather than organizational needs. Nowhere in this construction of meaning are learning deficiencies
problematized, nor are tensions between education and productivity acknowledged. Managers must reinforce the belief that "education is good."

This responsibility of constructing meaning offers the managers the
opportunity to enhance their own authority and job security while at the same
time acquiescing to organizational demands. The more the middle managers can
convince their superiors that employer-sponsored literacy education requires
dedicated management, the more certain is their authority and job security. Consequently, they mystify the processes somewhat, by reiterating the 'specialized'
nature of the expertise involved in managing the literacy programs. For example, one describes explaining to resistant supervisors "why ESL takes so long";
another speaks of the effort expended to hire "the right teacher." It is especially
important for those managers with state funding to construct meaning about the
program that is in keeping with the requirements of the grant, a time-consuming
bureaucratic task that calls for managerial discretion. The need for management
is further strengthened by hiring outsiders to teach and to create curriculum,
since such contract employees require managerial oversight if not belief management. In constructing meaning about the literacy programs, managers construct meaning about their own positions as being necessary, both inside and
outside the firm.

Boundary Spanning

Since basic education is not a usual activity of the work organization,
workplace literacy programs must be actively brought into work organizations,
usually first as an experiment. The stories that managers told of program inspi-
ration and inception varied greatly, but always involved someone in the organizational hierarchy recognizing either the literacy need or the potential offered
by employer-sponsored literacy education (or both), and taking a risk to implement such an innovation. Usually this meant extending beyond the boundaries of
the organization, as well as beyond the boundaries of the human resources or
training department. One manager told of going to a conference and hearing an
early adopter speak; another described reading an article in the local paper and
realizing that this solved her goal of trying to have an equitable array of educational opportunities. Adult education vendors themselves approached a number
of managers. Boundaries—private versus public, work versus school—became
blurred, as managers and educators, funding agencies and labor unions collabo-
rated to implement the education desired.

Once programs were in place, the various relationships with the teachers and state agencies also required ongoing managerial attention, continuing the

boundary spanning. Inside the organization, the managers needed to recruit students, an activity that required interaction with various areas of the organization. After classes began, the managers spent time negotiating with direct supervisors, other managers, and employee groups regarding time away from work, progress to be expected, and so forth. These activities offered additional opportunities to construct meaning about literacy, and they kept the managers busy.

While apparently a straightforward communication and coordination role, in the case of workplace literacy, boundary spanning necessitates special expertise concerning education. These managers must have the language and willingness to relate to those outside their organization and department, and the ability to translate outside interests (such as those of a private vendor of adult educational programs) in ways that make sense to the workplace. When asked what they learned from their involvement with literacy, several managers answered that they learned about education and its inherent difficulty. Said one,

> We take it for granted but they really appreciate the opportunity.
>
> *Human Resources Director,*
> *Small Hospital*

> There is no one best way [to teach adults]. There are lots of ways.
>
> *Training Manager,*
> *Retail Distribution Center*

Two, in fact, got so interested that they went back to graduate school to obtain degrees in adult learning. Managers acknowledged their specialty through language of inclusion, by saying, for example, "we in the training department," thereby differentiating themselves from the senior executive strata and the operational/line managers. Middle managers' authority is made somewhat secure given this type of demand for their expertise and managerial skill; it may be that their loss in position power is made up for by a gain in expert power.[3]

Gate-keeping

Control of access, referred to as gate-keeping, also strengthened the managers' security and position. One concern often associated with the blurring of responsibilities brought about by the new schoolhouse is that employers will control (and co-opt) education through their oversight of the curriculum content. As established earlier, this has not happened in the case of literacy. It appears that curriculum decisions have essentially been ceded to the adult educators. Middle managers (with a few exceptions) have little responsibility for or knowledge of curriculum or classroom practice, and they report that the executive level is disinterested in the content of learning as well. But these managers *do* control access to educational opportunity, perhaps more crucial than content in terms of the overall outcomes.

As gatekeepers, middle managers control critical aspects of employer-sponsored literacy education. To recap the various mechanisms: classes are bounded in time and duration, demand is encouraged but not met, enrollments are limited, managers decide how much education is enough, and support to attend classes is constrained. Many of these gate-keeping activities could be assigned to someone other than the middle manager responsible for training (a line manager perhaps), but have not been, because they are the means by which managers show the success of the employer-sponsored literacy education programming (i.e., by waiting lists). This control of access also further consolidates their power over those at lower levels.

So, the management of the workplace literacy program appears complex enough to require a person of authority, and an insider rather than a consultant. Still, the occurrence at Gary Electronics (see Chapter Six) should be kept in mind: there, a group of employees bypassed the human resources department and arranged their own specialized training. While such action is unlikely to be seen among low-level, barely literate employees, self-managed learning is a threat to the managers in the middle. They can forestall this threat by constructing meaning, boundary spanning, and gate-keeping. Such tasks can be justified as managerial, and may offer the manager a modicum of job security. Literacy programs allow managers to maintain their own professional boundaries: managerial power is assured if there are clear lines between those who manage education and those who need education.[4]

The Case for Fulfilling Work

It is important to note that managers find their involvement with workplace literacy to be a satisfying experience, so they gain more than job security from their managerial responsibilities. An earlier chapter established that managers liked being associated with firms that treated employees in a seemingly humane manner. It was also true that managers liked being associated with the specific activity of literacy. To a certain extent this was because the programs were seen to be a success. Managers said,

> I am thrilled at what we have been able to accomplish.
>
> *Training Director,*
> *Large Laundry Firm*

> It makes me feel good whenever I sit in graduation and every student is so completely thankful that we provided this for them. It makes it so much easier for them and it makes you feel good because they appreciated it so much.
>
> *Human Resources Director,*
> *Retail Grocery Chain*

And a third,

> Every organization should do this. It is very rewarding.
>
> *Training Manager,*
> *Large Teaching Hospital*

These reactions are somewhat predictable, given that these managers in many cases were the ones who proposed and championed the innovative programs, and they were also usually the ones responsible for implementation and evaluation. It is certainly in their best interests to find overall successful and positive outcomes, and to see evidence of such positive responses in the program participants.

What was remarkable was the emotional content of their responses, and the fact that this came through so strongly despite the fact that they were not asked "how did this make you feel?" This can be explained perhaps by the tenuous and stressful overall position of the middle manager.[5] Middle managers do not experience a great deal of professional or personal satisfaction in much of the day-to-day management work, caught as they are between the "order-givers" and the "order-takers." Therefore the opportunity to be involved in something as simple and universally appreciated as basic skills education appears to offer a rare and welcome opportunity for fulfillment. And, as will be established in the second half of the chapter, literacy education offers a site for resistance, and therefore is perhaps even more gratifying. Along with the satisfaction, however, managers experience challenges to their managerial authority, in part because education is unlike other benefits—it is difficult to control, and the outcome may be unexpected.

LEARNING TOO LITTLE, LEARNING TOO MUCH

The willingness to learn and change is by no means something that the manager can predict. Moreover, when learning *does* occur, managerial power and authority may well be threatened. Like parents sending their children off to school, managers allowing employees to attend class are ambivalent: they want to encourage independence and knowledge, but realize that such experiences will irrevocably alter their relationship and challenge their authority. Employees who resist learning as well as those who learn too much are a concern to managers interviewed.

Managerial control is quietly thwarted by those employees *not* willing to learn and change. One manager acknowledged that such learning was very difficult, while another realized that just because he embraced lifelong learning, he could not expect others to do so without sufficient incentive. The stigma of illiteracy also inhibited openness to learning. Comments reveal the managers' lack of control:

When you make it voluntary, you live with the consequences.

Director of Personnel,
Mid-sized Manufacturing Firm

You can only do so much—then they can do it themselves.

Training Director,
Small Hospital

You can lead them to water but you can't make them drink—
the same with education. The employee has to have initiative,
the employer can't force them.

Human Resources Manager,
Large Distribution Center

But managers rationalized this employee resistance as an inevitable outgrowth
of expecting individual responsibility. They were not terribly upset because such
uncooperative employees clearly were still in need of managers and management. While "living with the consequences" may be difficult for the managers to
accept, they can blame the employees for not upgrading skills, and consequently
can hold the employees responsible for productivity and overall competitive
success or lack thereof. This shifts responsibility away from the managers and
from the organization to the individual worker, a process integral to the development of the individualized employment contract, described in the previous
chapter.

At the same time, it is clear to both employee and manager that authority is being challenged, since "the employer can't force them," and no amount of
blaming the individual can truly absolve the manager of the presumed responsibility that goes along with the position/title of manager. Blaming the workers
will only go so far in protecting the middle manager. So these challenges to authority are a threat to the *power* of the human resources directors and training
managers in the middle layers of the organization, but they do not threaten their
position. As long as workers remain illiterate, managers will be deemed
necessary.

The unique nature of the educational opportunity results in a second
type of challenge to control. There is the possibility that employees will "learn
too much," as Chapter One described. This has various consequences: it may
result in enhanced employability for the individual worker, but also less need for
management as traditionally construed. One example of this has already been
described: the Gary Electronics workers who arranged for their own certificate
program (see beginning of Chapter Six). In another company, learning disrupted
workplace power relationships—new worker attitudes were not immediately
appreciated by the direct supervisors, as recounted by the middle manager:

[This company] used to operate under the paternalistic benevolent style—you know, "as long as you do what Dad says,

everyone will have fun on the vacation." That style was successful, to some degree, but when you start educating workers and want their involvement, then they start to challenge what "Dad" has to say. Some supervisors initially had some problems with this, but I tried to prevail upon them. I had to train them to value and encourage involvement and to recognize that to challenge their decisions in the company was not necessarily bad. Then they became a little more confident and able to deal with dissenting viewpoints. And that has been a battle.

Training and Development Director,
Multi-national Manufacturing Company

Educated workers are willing to challenge "Dad," and this alters cultural norms, behavioral expectations, and, by implication, the supervisor's authority. More education was then the result, since the training director had to create an educational program in order to "train them [supervisors] to value and encourage involvement." Here the human resources function was apparently strengthened rather than challenged by the "smarter" workers. Yet it was "a battle," indicating the new relationship was still challenged.

Whether they learn too much or too little, educated workers potentially affect the power balance in the organization. Yet even if the once illiterate workers earn a diploma, they are still at (or near) the bottom of the organizational hierarchy, and are still disadvantaged in the current environment. Middle managers remain organizationally necessary, even as "Dad" is perhaps less authoritarian. Aside from the tension generated by the learners' reactions to the literacy programs, these managers also experience tension as a result of unrealistic expectations from the executive tier.

PRESSURE FROM ABOVE

Literacy programs assist middle managers in their efforts to assert authority and to assure their continued employment. But this is not the intended purpose of such programs. As established earlier, the ostensible goal of employer-sponsored literacy education is to help firms contend with competitive pressures. But while the middle managers believe that this occurs, they cannot document clear organizational benefits. This leaves them in a problematic position versus senior managers, whose expectations may be unrealistic yet whose support is necessary. It is difficult to *prove* that literacy education programs are in the corporate interest, even though such programs exist within the halo of the education ideology. Literacy's benefit to the organization is typically indirect and it is difficult to control; literacy's more obvious benefits to the middle manager and the illiterate worker may not be adequate enough reason for senior managers to continue their support. Middle managers must therefore respond to the pressure from above in such a way that convinces the top tier that literacy programs matter, while at the same time remaining true to what they themselves believe as to the benefits of literacy beyond the corporate interest. This can be rather tricky—yet the managers with whom I spoke showed creativity and courage in their subtle resistance.

RESISTING THE CORPORATE INTEREST

Middle managers are aware of the tension between learning that meets individual needs and learning that meets business or organizational needs—"in-house benefits as opposed to external benefits," as one recounted. This tension is openly discussed. One manager spoke about the role of education in fostering self-esteem and the fact that "business" managers didn't share her beliefs:

> So when I say yes, self-esteem is very big when it comes to HR and training and development, that doesn't mean that the business managers feel the same way.
>
> *Human Resources Director,*
> *Multi-state Bank*

Along the same lines, the training director of a community hospital said, "For human resources, it is exciting to treat people from a broader perspective." The implication is that the larger organization treats people too narrowly—as interchangeable parts rather than as humans who would appreciate the chance to be educated. Consequently, managers make decisions that are not necessarily in the corporate interest, further blurring the boundaries of the new schoolhouse.

Personal versus Business Goals

Several managers described the conflict they felt between the organization's goals and their own views with regard to education. They inevitably used the word "personal" in their comments pertaining to this tension, though the question did not use that term or explicitly direct them to differentiate their personal views from those of the organization. These feelings were close to the surface:

> No matter how many days I am sort of cursing the corporation, I can say that they did stand by these programs. I am not saying that the company is out there being altruistic. It says that the company is making an investment in its own bottom line.
>
> *Training Manager,*
> *Large Bank*

> Social reasons are a personal incentive, yet they are not
> sellable due to cost consciousness. Other managers are won-
> derfully supportive.
>
> *Human Resources Manager,*
> *Small Hospital*

By clearly differentiating their "personal" views from those of the "business,"
the respondents distanced themselves from the organizational goals and expressed ambivalence. They are "cursing the corporation" and criticizing the corporate "cost-consciousness" while at the same time expressing gratitude that
programs can continue and praising the support of other managers. Others were
less equivocal:

> My personal feeling is that education is never wasted. From
> the hospital's point of view, if it's not job related, they don't
> see a big commitment.
>
> *Manager of Continuing Education,*
> *Large Hospital*

In some cases, personal and organizational goals were congruent:

> My personal philosophy is pro-education. This is strongly
> supported by my boss and the top tier.
>
> *Human Resources Director,*
> *Retail Distribution Center*

> Personally, I feel that companies need to be more community
> minded and responsible, and I convinced the VP. But [the
> original motive] was for business.
>
> *Training Director,*
> *Community Hospital*

These managers were cognizant of their limited power, as they noted the crucial
role played by the support from above, the "boss" and "VP." Yet again, both
used the word "personal," implying a distinction between their humane impulses
and the demands of the business environment. Resistance took the form of
"convincing the VP," showing autonomy in the face of coercive pressures, and
revealing a sense of efficacy that was not shared by all. The tenuousness of the
educational endeavor in the face of business pressures and general impatience is
apparent here, as is the pressure on the individual manager to mediate between
short- and long-term business goals.

Social Interests

A few middle managers deviate even further from business goals, by seeing their role as helping those less fortunate, especially immigrant workers. One manager said (emphasis added),

> I learned that education really opens doors and I am lucky to have personally had the opportunity. There are so many obstacles for *poor people*—education really makes people feel better about themselves and helps to level the playing field.
>
> *Human Resources VP,*
> *Electronics Manufacturer*

By acknowledging a sense of responsibility to poor people, this manager was somewhat unusual, but not alone. There may be a proclivity as human resource specialists to feel some responsibility for lower level workers, though this is by no means universal. It was unclear whether such views were shared by senior management—the use of the first person singular implies that these are personal views only.

Another manager articulated a more global conflict, juxtaposing her political views about immigrants with those of the rest of the nation. She said:

> I am a liberal democrat, so I say yes, the employer must take responsibility for literacy education, but the feeling of the nation is definitely not. The feeling of the nation is if you have come to this country, you've got to do it on your own. What I would like and what the rest of the world would do is in conflict.
>
> *Director of Human Resources,*
> *Small Institutional Laundry*

Despite her protestations concerning the national backlash against immigrant workers, this manager has been able to accomplish what she "would like" even in an environment not necessarily conducive to liberal views, creating an intriguing site for tempered resistance. Further conversation revealed her dismay about the other changes in the employment relationship—she wanted her company to retain its paternalistic attitude and culture. Her goal is "to make it easier for these employees to get a piece of the pie," and she realizes that they will never get it "without English." When asked what she learned from her involvement with literacy education, she said that she was "very pleased to see that employers do care about employees." Yet she does not acknowledge that the employers' "caring" does not extend to better wages or to more significant educational interventions. Again, the educational programs take on a value far greater than their monetary equivalence.

The above examples are hardly indications of overt confrontation, but such attitudes and actions nonetheless are a challenge to the organization on two levels: first, except in social service agencies, organizational goals do not revolve around helping the needy. So those who believe in such actions are placing their personal social consciences ahead of the employer's needs. Such managers believe in the education solution even if it is not necessarily in the corporate interest. This degree of independent action is unexpected, which is probably why it is unnoticed and allowed to continue. Second, from a broader perspective, the growing numbers of immigrant workers might threaten organizations. Though many companies today assert that they are valuing and embracing diversity for business reasons, the idea of a truly multi-cultural/multi-ethnic senior (or even middle) level is still not fully embraced. So the realization that individual managers are taking such risks for lower level employees reveals managerial agency beyond what economistic logic or institutional theory would suggest.[6]

It seems that the middle managers are aware of the intangible nature of the organizational (not to mention individual and societal) benefits that derive from employer-sponsored literacy education, yet cannot use these personal beliefs to convince senior management of their efficacy. So they argue for literacy programs using other techniques. Like educators forced to play the Franklin card (described in Chapter One), middle managers must stress pragmatic benefits while quietly supporting a broad curriculum. To quote one manager, he knows "what's right" about the education they offer, but also recognizes the need to be artful in convincing others to blur institutional boundaries and support workplace education.

Managerial Power and the Greater Good

In search of mobility for the laboring classes, educational opportunity for immigrant workers, and/or social responsibility for corporations, it seems that these managers are exhibiting a degree of managerial power in resistance to the ubiquitous productivity and profit pressures from above. They have used their autonomy not to outwardly challenge the senior management dictates; indeed, they can surely justify their literacy expenditures as having corporate benefits (though they won't are not able to "prove it" using any hard numbers). Rather, their authority and autonomy have been quietly marshaled for a greater good, a good that benefits the organization, the worker, and the managers themselves. Yet the question remains, if the managers are indeed so powerful, why don't they do more? Specifically, why can't they increase the class hours to allow adequate learning intensity? And why don't they try to obtain fairer compensation for those low-level workers now taking on additional responsibilities? Clearly, there are limits to managerial power and resistance, limits inherent in the larger system. These limits must be taken seriously in understanding the new schoolhouse, and particularly with regard to literacy policy.

MANAGERS, AGENCY, AND BOUNDARY BLURRING

Building upon the new contract discussion in Chapter Six, it appears that by ultimately individualizing the responsibility for the firm's competitive success, literacy programs serve the managers well. If they can blame the employees for not learning despite having opportunities available, then they remove the responsibility from themselves, while at the same time assuring that they stay employed and that the managerial hierarchy remains intact. This is not to say that these managers set out to be self-serving—managers are motivated to provide literacy education due to humanitarian concerns, or because they have been convinced of its importance and value. Yet they do benefit: materially, emotionally, and ideologically. In several ways, the interests of managers and workers are aligned through the provision of education, as education allows them a site for opposing and mediating senior management demands in the face of ongoing organizational turbulence. These themes of humane treatment of employees, managerial expertise as a source of power, and continued covert challenges to business goals are crucial in understanding the impact of the new schoolhouse.

In closing, I suggest that this focus on the individual manager gives the employer a face and a voice, and reminds us that the organization is indeed full of people, with potential to make humane decisions, as well as self-serving ones. The insertion of individual voices into the discussion of the disembodied new schoolhouse demonstrates that policies can be negotiated, and that contradictory interests can be creatively accommodated. The middle manager who resists being controlled by executives, preserves authority alongside an empowered workforce, and justifies continued employment during a time of management layoffs allows insight into the possibilities for individual agency in the face of structural forces.

NOTES

1. The disproportionate loss of managerial jobs has been alleged by many but finally has been persuasively documented by Paul Osterman in *Securing Prosperity: The American Labor Market: How It Has Changed and What to Do about It* (Princeton, NJ: Princeton University Press, 1999).

2. This phrase is from the title of a book that provided a range of useful insights as I considered the contradictions inherent in the work of the middle manager. See Vicki B. Smith, *Managing in the Corporate Interest: Control and Resistance in an American Bank* (Berkeley: University of California Press, 1990).

3. John R. French and Bertram Raven, "The Bases of Social Power," on *Group Dynamics,* edited by Dorwin Cartwrithg and Alvin Zander (New York: Harper and Row, 1968), building on the work of Max Weber, created a typology of interpersonal power. They identified five bases: reward, coercive, legitimate, referent, and expert. Legitimate power would be that held by the middle manager by virtue of his or her position within the organizational hierarchy. Social theorists suggest that as organizations flatten, other types of power will grow in importance. Most attention is given to expertise as the power

base in ascendance, given the technological and complex nature of organizational changes. A book of the same title argues that we are "in an age of experts" (Brint 1994).

4. Along the same lines, Gowen (1992:131) discussed the use of literacy classes by workers to maintain boundaries between and among the "in groups" and others in the workplace, arguing that the contribution of literacy to the larger structure of the organization must be taken into account.

5. Smith, in *Managing in the Corporate Interest* (1990) discusses the plight of those in the middle. Charles Heckscher also discusses their stressful situation in *White-Collar Blues* (New York: Basic Books, 1995). A dire portrait is painted by Robert Jackall in *Moral Mazes: The World of Corporate Managers* (New York: Oxford University Press, 1988).

6. This process might be theorized as bringing agency into the institutionalization process. In their "Introduction" to *The New Institutionalism in Organizational Analysis* (1991), Powell and DiMaggio suggest that this is a necessary development in what they refer to as a "Theory of Practical Action." See their discussions of the micro foundations of macro process, on pp. 16 and especially 22–27. This site of the new schoolhouse contributes to the understanding of institutionalization by focusing on two key groups of actors: the middle managers discussed here, and the adult educators, analyzed earlier. By focusing on their actions, the systemic changes become understandable and less oblique.

8

Literacy, Managers, and Belief: Engaging the Contradictions

In considering the causes and consequences of workplace literacy education, it has become clear that this activity is neither the "win-win" scenario proposed by policymakers, nor the capitulation to employer demands expected by critics of corporations. Rather, middle managers and cultural beliefs about education, among other factors, have created workplace literacy programs that have *both* costs and benefits, for individuals, organizations, and society. In this chapter, I will examine these contradictory findings in order to make recommendations for literacy policy and for employers involved in such programs. I will also return to the question of ideology, and propose alternate beliefs that are potentially more accurate and more just.

WHO BENEFITS?

Middle managers, adult educators, and workers all appear to benefit from the provision of literacy at work. On the most basic level, the managers profit from continued employment, since educational programs require management. Second, they gain societal approbation for their association with such a culturally valued activity as education. Third, the provision of education allows managers to differentiate themselves from the uneducated and illiterate, thus strengthening the managerial power structure and assuring their continued authority. Additionally, these programs offer managers an opportunity to resist unrealistic demands from the executive level, since managers use the illiteracy of workers and the subsequent need for worker education to simultaneously appear to be working towards a more productive workforce, while at the same time deflecting unrealistic executive expectations. A key outcome of this resistance is that senior and middle managers avoid being blamed for organizational problems. Paradoxically, managers have much to gain from illiterate employees and from attempts to decrease illiteracy. Much like managers, adult educators obtain continued employment, professional satisfaction, and legitimacy through their involvement with employer-sponsored literacy. The workplace classroom assists their professionalization project, since they must use their growing expertise and power to navigate the cultural differences between the worlds of education and business. Not surprisingly, the illiterate employees benefit from the workplace literacy program. Modernity demands literacy, or at least the appearance of such, and literate employees gain in pay and promotional opportunity within the firm, particularly if they have obtained a diploma or equivalent credential. Furthermore, as reported, the personal benefits extend beyond cognitive and material gains. Attitudinal changes, particularly enhanced self-esteem, no doubt spill over to nonwork activities, allowing the workers' families and communities to benefit from the positive attitude.

The benefits to the work organization are highly touted, although not well proven. Belief outweighs empirical evidence. Most important, though not explicitly, it appears that workplace literacy programs are a relatively inexpensive way to obtain a higher skilled, loyal, yet still low-wage workforce, a workforce that possesses the requisite positive job attitudes as well as seemingly improved literacy. The organization also benefits symbolically. First, moral legitimacy results from the highly valued education solution, along with the appearance of supplying employability. Second, taking on the responsibility for education serves to exempt the firm from other responsibilities, such as employment security and accountability for productivity. Through the provision of literacy and other educational opportunities, the employer communicates to the employee, "Don't depend on us, depend on yourself." This message reinforces the individualistic thrust of the new employment contract, while at the same time relieving the organization of responsibility for continued employment. In this way, workplace literacy programs differ significantly from benefits such as daycare or dental insurance that reinforce the paternalistic employment relationship. Finally, while appearing to equip the firm with the flexibility to adapt to changing external conditions, the provision of literacy concurrently offers stability, in that the organizational hierarchy remains intact once literacy deficits have been acknowledged and the need for the middle management strata has been reiterated.

Society benefits at various levels as a result of the belief that literacy levels and job performance improves. Rhetorically, jobs are kept from going offshore or being eliminated altogether, a literate citizenry can share more thoughtfully in a participatory democracy, and the social problems associated with illiteracy, competitiveness, and school failure are ameliorated. The public sector is relieved of its burden to educate, in part, and those proponents of private solutions to social problems laud the employers' active involvement.

Furthermore, the cross-sectoral efforts that typify most workplace literacy programs serve to foster interdependence and result in greater societal cohesion. Yet there are costs, often obscured by the multiple benefits as well as by the unquestioned belief that "education is good."

UNREALISTIC EXPECTATIONS: COSTS ASSOCIATED WITH EMPLOYER-SPONSORED EDUCATION

The "wins" for individuals, organizations, and the society are mitigated by less obvious losses. While the symbolic value of literacy education is great, the reality is that most programs fall far short of what is required to bring the workforce up to more than minimal levels of functional competence. Students improve their English, and may even earn a high school diploma, but they are by no means being educated adequately enough to move out of the ranks of the working poor. Employability is a convenient myth. Little real skill acquisition is possible from a literacy class that meets for a few hours a week, even if it is available to workers for several years. Perhaps in comparison with the Mexican or Thai workforces, these literacy levels are adequate to do the job—and maybe that is what matters to employers, but these students are not the knowledge workers or the symbolic analysts of the high-wage, high-skill economy so promoted by policy makers. Most of these workers can barely make a living wage even *with* their GEDs and English competency. Managers repeatedly reported that students had to go to second or third jobs after their hospital or manufacturing shifts, making it impossible to continue their education on their own time. So while the opportunity to learn basic skills at work is laudable, the contribution to individual mobility and overall economic competitiveness likely results from the symbolic rather than educational outcomes of employer-sponsored literacy. And the fact that workplace literacy does not always live up to its promises is blamed on the worker, rather than on the structure of the program.

This individualization of responsibility has further negative impact. If workers accept that their individual educational deficiencies are the justification for their continued low pay and low status, then they are unlikely to protest structural unfairness. Workers' positive attitudes towards their jobs (defined as being aligned with their employers), result in enhanced consent, and consequently will diminish oppositional consciousness. Labor power is also weakened as the new contract replaces job security with token educational opportunity. And by blaming the victim, rather than the system, employers escape responsibility on both real and symbolic terms. Dominant ideology is not challenged, as literacy programs maintain inequities while ostensibly offering mobility and possibility.

While the most significant costs are to the barely literate workers, middle managers can be considered disadvantaged, too, due to their involvement in workplace literacy programs. The threat of the educated worker adds to managerial insecurity, decreasing their sense of freedom and making them less likely to take risks. Those who have the insight to realize the paltry nature of their firm's workplace education efforts may also pay a price in terms of cynicism or disaffection. The thesis that middle managers have become proletarianized is not borne out by this analysis, though the fact that they work to assure that the hierarchy remains stable suggests that their positions are not as powerful as they once were. The new economy and the new contract appear to only minimally affect these managers, stuck as they are in the middle of their organizations, as well as in the midst of structural changes that they cannot control.

The belief in the education solution has costs for the employer, as well. Organizational problems will not be solved by these educational programs alone. Attention to literacy obscures scrutiny of the structural economic problems that truly threaten the firm (and its employees at all levels). By allowing blame to be shifted to these programs or to the illiterate workers, senior executives as well as middle managers avoid confronting other explanations for their companies' dilemmas. Organizations do not benefit from the privatization of adult education, either, since if they were to truly take on the responsibility for educational programming, costs would be prohibitive and work disruptions would be great. Firms increase their vulnerability as they seek the moral legitimacy accorded the schoolhouse role; without economic success to back up this strategy, it may backfire.

From a societal perspective, employer-sponsored literacy education can also be seen as solidifying systemic *inequities,* even as it purports to do otherwise. Workplace literacy programs as currently construed cannot possibly result in the knowledge and skills supposedly in demand in the current economy. The limited nature of the education that is offered in workplace literacy programs *contributes* to the perpetuation of structural inequalities even as stability is enhanced. A society stabilized yet polarized is ultimately weak, as well as unjust.

THE SNAPSHOT AND THE LONG TERM

These costs and benefits might be challenged with respect to the temporal nature of the findings. It is possible that the workplace literacy programs described here are an anomaly, another short-lived human resources fad. Indeed, several respondents cited waning interest, asserting that the employers' need for such programs peaked during the mid-1990s with high employment rates and restricted immigration. However, that this particular innovation takes the form of *education* suggests an organizational innovation of more than temporary significance, even if the programs themselves are short-lived. I believe that the phenomenon will have a lasting effect for several reasons: first, the employer has expanded its acceptable and/or expected sphere of interest, with unacknowledged historical precedent, precedent that only becomes stronger as each generation discovers it "anew." The state role has changed to one of collaboration with the private sector, and government actively recruits employer involvement. Both public and private sectors seem to accept this shift in responsibility for literacy education, though not without grumbling and resistance from the employers. From the theoretical perspective as well, workplace literacy programs should be understood as being more than just another human resources fad. As institutional theory suggests, employers and employees alike have come to take the value of the new schoolhouse for granted, just as education in the larger society is unquestioned. Employees have been become accustomed to this particular model of learning at work, and managers are enthused, so new norms have been created. At the same time, a new professional specialty has been solidified, and adult educators will continue to advocate for their expertise and autonomy. These findings are particularly instructive with regard to the consequences of private sponsorship: schooling in workplaces looks increasingly like schooling in the public sector (as institutional theory suggests). If this is the case, then the new schoolhouse might simply be an example of fund shifting, and the boundary blurring that occurs may be of little consequence.

Should these employer-sponsored literacy education programs prove to be anomalous, they still illuminate consequential, though not yet well understood, transitions in the post-industrial era. This book offers only a snapshot of an ongoing social phenomenon. A more complete understanding of the complex relationship between work and learning would entail a longitudinal study of firms, workers, and managers with attention to such factors as productivity, job satisfaction, pay, and career movement as they relate to education and learning. Also, ongoing study of privatization is needed, with attention to other settings and other temporal periods.

ADDRESSING THE INEQUITIES OF THE EDUCATION SOLUTION

What then is to be done? Do the costs of continued illiteracy and its contribution to the growing gap between rich and poor outweigh the benefits of workplace education? Schooling is like Mom and apple pie—no one wants to call it into question, especially if that would mean *less* rather than more education. Yet is the new schoolhouse an appropriate venue for basic skills?   More important, *should* such boundary blurring continue?   The answer to these questions is "yes, but. . . ."

The recommendations that follow arise from the belief that complex social problems (such as illiteracy and inequality) must be tackled from multiple angles. There are a range of effective policies that might be crafted; but the ideological blinders must be removed, narrow interests thwarted, earlier mistakes acknowledged, and the political will summoned.

The basic skills education that employers provide *is* beneficial for those employees fortunate enough to be offered such opportunities. For the most part, this is education in the broadest sense, designed not just for work but transferable to home or community, or from one workplace to another. With regard to what is learned, this new schoolhouse is not very different from the old schoolhouse, only perhaps more conveniently located. It does not appear that the educational content is being co-opted by work-related needs, which is the good news. Thus *employer-sponsored literacy programs should continue*. Costs to employers are not great, and benefits appear to be diverse and multiple.

However, as established above, intensity is inadequate. Employers who decide that their role now includes much more education and training need to be cognizant of the fact that genuine education must be a long-term commitment. Intensity (many hours, regularly offered) matters, not only for literacy but also for other types of learning. Such commitment is expensive, and employers can expect resistance on many levels: from workers, supervisors, managers, senior management, the board of directors, and investors. Nevertheless, the recommendation is that *firms significantly increase the amount of time devoted to literacy education*, and to other types of broad learning that may have benefits beyond the specific task.

The larger concern is that workplace efforts barely address the US literacy problem in its magnitude. Very few people, relative to the need, are able to take advantage of current opportunities. First, workplace education is limited to those with permanent workforce attachments, a declining proportion of the entire labor pool and a relatively small segment of the unskilled labor force. Those who work part time or as contract workers are usually ineligible, as are most employees in the franchise and retail sectors. Therefore, *employers must expand the scope of existing efforts to include part-time and temporary workers. Employers in noncore firms should be encouraged to sponsor educational programs*. Second, within the small percentage of firms that do offer programs, managers estimate that barely half of those who need the education are attending, due to various personal and organizational constraints. So, *employers should create mechanisms to assure that employees are able to attend classes in the workplace*. Third, it is estimated that only 20% of all U.S. employers currently sponsor workplace education, not because they perceive that there is no need, but because they are unaware of how to initiate such programs, or are unwilling/unable to commit necessary resources. Consequently, *efforts to increase employer-sponsored literacy programs should continue*. This is especially important as welfare reform has sent more adults directly into the workplace regardless of their skills, education, or literacy levels.

WHO SHOULD BE RESPONSIBLE? RECOMMENDATIONS FOR PUBLIC AND PRIVATE SECTORS

The above recommendations encourage continued, enlarged private sector involvement in the provision of literacy education. This is justified by the realization that workplace literacy programs are pragmatic, are politically expedient, and do not appear to negatively affect educational content. Yet employers alone cannot be held responsible. In terms of the overall need for literacy education in this country, existing workplace and community programs are serving only a small proportion. Therefore, a recommendation to *increase the scope of all literacy education efforts* is the primary, and not surprising, suggestion resulting from this research. Adults need more classes, more programs, and more support services. Additional resources are called for: material and political, private and public.

With regard to the concerns about private control of such a basic need, findings suggest that boundary blurring is more complex than it first appears. Privatization is negotiated by the various and occasionally conflicting interests of the individuals involved: students, teachers, and managers influence the employer's power over the provision of literacy education. Moreover, there are systemic checks and balances in this current arrangement, resulting from the professionals involved, the participative model of education employed, and government guidelines. Nonetheless, because employer power dwarfs that of any group of individuals, I suggest that the state must be involved in order to assure fairness and quality. *The public sector must increase its oversight and support of employer-sponsored literacy.* For example, the state can continue its efforts to certify adult educators and assure that teachers have professional benefits and ongoing development; can require that curriculum be broadly construed and learner-centered rather than workplace specific; can assist in paying employees for classroom attendance; and provide for long-term rather than quick-fix approaches.

Furthermore, if responsibility for adult literacy is to be shared by the private and public sectors, employers and business leaders have a role to play in assuring that literacy concerns are given prominence in the national debate. Rather than simply reacting to presumed social conditions (i.e., "we have no choice"), employers must proactively involve themselves in changing attitudes and improving services to those who lack basic literacy. Broad organizational and societal benefits will result from such long-term policies. Specifically, employers should:

- understand the complexity of the basic skill acquisition process for adults and not expect immediate transformative effects at the academic level
- allocate an adequate amount of time for literacy learning (at least two classes per week)
- work to reduce stigma associated with illiteracy at work and in the broader society
- lobby for community as well as workplace spending
- participate in partnerships with community agencies; open onsite literacy programs to neighborhoods and families
- hire those with expertise in the field of adult education; listen to their advice
- tie literacy and other ongoing skill development training to internal job ladders or growing fields outside the firm; teach employability skills

THE SOCIOLOGICAL CHALLENGE

The core contradiction of the workplace literacy program is that it improves individual prospects yet solidifies structural inequities. In "solving" individual and organizational problems, employer-sponsored education worsens social problems. The conundrum is that the connection between the individual and the social is obscured by the educational process itself; and education is the usual medium for alerting people to these essential connections. The challenge for the sociologist and the activist is to make this connection explicit, and to create an approach to social justice that fuses individual and social interests. To reiterate:

Undue focus on education as solution serves to divert attention from the economic system as a whole. Capitalism is a system that creates obvious winners and losers, and late capitalism has the potential to exploit even while purporting to empower. Until the flaws in the system, not the ostensible flaws in the individual, are acknowledged and addressed, there is little hope that the promise of an educated citizenry can be fully realized. The dominant ideology allows the persistence of the status quo, a status quo that at present is remarkably inequitable.

Overemphasis on education also obscures the stark fact that there are not enough good jobs. Literacy can indeed assist in workforce development, but this is merely a supply side perspective that ignores the other half the equation. In the current economy, the jobs with adequate pay, benefits, and opportunities for advancement simply do not exist. Again, such good jobs are increasingly scarce for even the most credentialed individual. It appears that until there is sufficient demand, there will be an oversupply of labor, literate or not.

Reliance on education as a solution often presumes, incorrectly, that all education is the same. As Socrates suggested, the purpose of the liberal education is to prepare one for an unpredictable future. Consequently a broad definition of literacy must prevail. Yet as stated above, a broad interpretation of education is necessary in order to prepare workers for an uncertain future. The problem with using the pragmatic rationale to justify education is that such liberal ideals may be lost, with possibilities for anything but the narrowest learning effectively foreclosed. Moreover, the time allotted to literacy education offered by employers is currently truncated and therefore inadequate.

As the new schoolhouse is brought out of the shadows, it becomes clear that social justice concerns are at the core of the answers to the question, "who benefits?" The answers are complex and ambiguous, but not so elusive that definite recommendations cannot be made. The most significant concern with respect to workplace literacy programs is that they create the appearance that larger social and economic problems are being solved, at the same time denying attention to the underlying causes and obscuring noneducational solutions. Consequently, policy discussions cannot be limited to literacy, workforce development, or competitiveness. Rather, a discussion must be engaged as to the type of world we want to live in, and the place of work and learning in that world. It is clear that the tensions between work and learning, business and education, the economy and the state are likely to continue, although in ever evolving forms. Given this, the confluence of business and social interests must continue to be scrutinized. The consequences, as demonstrated, are great, not only for the individuals involved in workplace literacy—workers, teachers, and managers—but for all of us.

Bibliography

Abbott, Andrew. *The System of Professions: An Essay on the Division of Expert Labor.* Chicago: University of Chicago Press, 1988.

A.L.L. Points Bulletin, Washington, DC: Division of Adult Education and Literacy, Office of Vocational and Adult Education, U.S. Dept. of Education, (November 18, 1999).

all write news 10, no. 5. Boston: Adult Literacy Resource Institute (March/April 1994): 1, 4.

Anderson, Claire J. "Corporate Social Responsibility and Worker Skills: An Examination of Corporate Responses to Work Place Illiteracy." *Journal of Business Ethics* 12 (1993): 281-292.

Aronowitz, Stanley and Henry Giroux. *Education Still Under Siege: The Conservative, Liberal, and Radical Debate Over Schooling.* Second Edition. Westport, CT: Bergin & Garvey, 1993.

Arrow, Kenneth, Samuel Bowles, and Steven Durlauf, eds. *Meritocracy and Economic Inequality.* Princeton, NJ: Princeton University Press, 2000.

Bassi, Laurie J. *Smart Workers, Smart Work.* Washington, DC: Southport Institute for Policy Analysis, 1992.

Bassi, Laurie J. "Workplace Education for Hourly Workers." *Journal of Policy Analysis and Management* 13, no. 1 (1994): 55-74.

Becker, Gary E. *Human Capital: A Theoretical and Empirical Analysis with Special Reference to Education,* Second Edition. New York: Columbia University Press, 1975.

Beder, Hal. *Adult Literacy: Issues for Policy and Practice.* Malabar, FL: Krieger, 1991.

Bell, Daniel. *Coming of the Post-Industrial Society.* New York: Basic Books, 1973.

Bellah, Robert, Richard Madsen, William M. Sullivan, Ann Swidler, and Steven M. Tipton. *Habits of the Heart: Individualism and Commitment in American Life.* Berkeley: University of California Press, 1985.

Berg, Ivar. *Education and Jobs: The Great Training Robbery.* New York: Praeger, 1970.

Berger, Peter L. *Invitation to Sociology.* New York: Doubleday/Anchor, 1963.

Bidwell, Charles E. and Noah E. Friedkin. "The Sociology of Education." In *The Encyclopedia of Sociology,* edited by Neil J. Smelser. Newbury Park, CA: Sage Publications, 1988.

Blanton, Kimberly. "Study Details Immigrants' Importance." *Boston Globe.* (November 17, 1999).

Blau, Peter. *Exchange and Power in Social Life.* New York: Wiley, 1964.

Bloom, Michael R. and Brenda Lafleur. *Turning Skills into Profit.* New York: The Conference Board, 1999.

Bourdieu, Pierre and Jean-Claude Passeron. *Reproduction in Education, Society, and Culture.* Translated by Richard Nice. Beverly Hills: Sage, 1977.

Bowles, Samuel and Herbert Gintis. *Schooling in Capitalist America: Educational Reform and Contradictions in Economic Life.* New York: Basic Books, 1976.

Boyle, Mary-Ellen. "Immigrant Workers and the Shadow Education System." *Education Policy* 13 (1999): 251-279.

Branscombe, Lewis M. and Paul C. Gilmore. "Education in Private Industry." *Daedalus,* (Winter 1975): 222-233.

Brint, Steven. *In an Age of Experts: The Changing Role of Professionals in* Politics and Public Life. Princeton, NJ: Princeton University Press, 1994.

Brint, Steven and Jerome Karabel. *The Diverted Dream: Community Colleges and the Promise of Educational Opportunity in America, 1900-1985.* New York: Oxford University Press, 1989.

Brown, David K. *Degrees of Control: A Sociology of Educational Expansion and Occupational Credentialism.* New York: Teachers College Press, 1995.

Bruner, Jerome. "Introduction." In *Literacy: An Overview by Fourteen Experts,* edited by Stephen R. Graubard. New York: Hill and Wang, 1991.

Burawoy, Michael. *Manufacturing Consent: Changes in the Labor Process Under Monopoly Capitalism.* Chicago: University of Chicago Press, 1979.

Bureau of the Census, "The American Community Survey: Your Community's Key To The Future." Washington, DC: U.S. Department of Commerce, Economics and Statistics Administration, 1997.

Cappelli, Peter. "Rethinking the 'Skills Gap.' " *California Management Review* 37, no. 4 (1995): 108-124.

Cappelli, Peter and Nikolai Rogovsky. "New Work Systems and Skill Requirements." *International Labour Review* 133, no. 2 (1994): 205-220.

Cappelli, Peter, Laurie Bassi, Harry Katz, David Knoke, Paul Osterman, and Michael Useem. *Change at Work.* New York: Oxford University Press, 1997.

Carnevale, Anthony P. and Leila J. Gainer. *The Learning Enterprise.* Washington, DC: The American Society for Training and Development and the U.S. Department of Labor, 1989.

Carnevale, Anthony P., Leila J. Gainer, and Ann S. Meltzer. *Workplace Basics.* San Francisco: Jossey-Bass, 1990.

Carnevale, Anthony P., Leila J. Gainer, and Janice Vaillet. *Training in America: The Organizational and Strategic Role.* San Francisco: Jossey-Bass, 1990.

Castells, Manuel. *The Rise of the Network Society.* Oxford: Blackwell, 1996.

Chilton, Kenneth and Murray Weidenbaum. *A New Social Contract for the American Workplace: From Paternalism to Partnering.* St. Louis Center for the Study of American Business, Policy Study Number 123, 1994.

Chisman, Forrest P. *Jump Start: The Federal Role in Adult Literacy.* Washington, DC: Southport Institute for Policy Analysis, 1989.

Chisman, Forrest P. *The Missing Link: Workplace Education in Small Business*. Washington, DC: Southport Institute for Policy Analysis, 1992.

Clark, Burton. "The 'Cooling-Out' Function in Higher Education." In *Education, Economy and Society,* edited by A. H. Halsey, et al., 513-521. New York: Free Press, 1961.

Collins, Sheila. "Workplace Literacy: Corporate Tool or Worker Empowerment?" *Social Policy* (Summer 1989): 26-30.

Craig, Robert L. and Christine J. Evers. "Employers and Educators: The Shadow Education System." In *Business and Higher Education: Toward a New Alliance,* edited by Gerard G. Gold. San Francisco: Jossey-Bass, 1981.

Darrah, Charles N. *Learning and Work: An Exploration in Industrial Ethnograpy.* New York: Garland Publishers, 1996.

Derber, Charles, William Schwartz, and Yale Magrass. *Power in the Highest Degree: Professionals and the Rise of the New Mandarin Order.* New York: Oxford University Press, 1990.

DiMaggio, Paul J. and Walter W. Powell. "The Iron Cage Revisited: Institutional Isomorphism and Collective Rationality in Organizational Fields." *American Sociological Review* (April 1983): 147-160.

DiTomaso, Nancy and Judith J. Friedman. "A Sociological Commentary on Workforce 2000." In *The New Modern Times,* edited by David B. Bills, 207-233. Albany: State University of New York Press, 1995.

Doeringer, Peter B. "The Future of Workplace Productivity Systems." Presented at the Academy of Management Meetings, Human Resources Division, Atlanta, Georgia, August 10, 1993.

Dore, Ronald Philip. *The Diploma Disease: Education, Qualification, and Development.* Berkeley: University of California Press, 1976.

Dudley, Katherine. *The End of the Line.* Chicago: University of Chicago, 1994.

Edwards, Richard. *Contested Terrain: The Transformation of the Workplace in the Twentieth Century.* New York: Basic Books, 1979.

Eggleston, J. *The Sociology of the School Curriculum.* London: Routledge & Kegan, 1977.

Ettore, Barbara. "Empty Promises: The New Employment Contract." *Management Review* 7, no. 85 (1996): 16.

Eurich, Nell P. *Corporate Classrooms: The Learning Business.* Princeton, NJ: Princeton University Press, 1985.

Eurich, Nell P. *The Learning Industry: Education For Adult Workers.* Princeton, NJ: Princeton University Press, 1990.

First Findings From The EQW National Employer Survey. Washington, DC: U.S. Dept. of Education, Office of Educational Research and Improvement, Educational Resources Information Center, 1995.

Fisher, Bernice M. *Industrial Education: American Ideals and Institutions.* Madison: University of Wisconsin Press, 1967.

Freire, Paolo. *Pedagogy of the Oppressed.* New York: Seabury, 1974.

Freire, Paolo. *Pedagogy of Hope.* New York: Continuum, 1992.

French, John R. and Bertram Raven. "The Bases of Social Power." In *Group Dynamics,* edited by Dorwin Cartwright and Alvin Zander. New York: Harper and Row, 1968.

Fuller, Bruce and Richard F. Elmore, eds. *Who Chooses? Who Loses? Culture, Institutions, and the Unequal Effects of School Choice.* New York: Teachers College Press, 1996.

Gee, James Paul, Glynda Hull, and Colin Lankshear. *The New Work Order: Behind the Language of the New Capitalism.* Boulder, CO: Westview Press, 1996.

Ghoshal, Sumantra and Christopher A. Bartlett. *The Individualized Corporation.* New York: Harper Business, 1997.

Giroux, Henry. *Teachers as Intellectuals: Toward a Critical Pedagogy of Learning.* Hadley, MA: Bergin and Garvey, 1988.

Giroux, Henry. *Border Crossings: Cultural Workers and the Politics of Education.* New York: Routledge, 1992.

Giroux, Henry A. "What Is Literacy?" In *Becoming Political: Readings and Writings in the Politics of Literacy Education.* Compiled by Patrick Shannon. Portsmouth, NH: Heinemann, 1992.

Gowen, Sheryl. *The Politics of Workplace Literacy.* New York: Teachers College Press, 1992.

Grant, Gerald. *The World We Created at Hamilton High.* Cambridge: Harvard University Press, 1988.

Guidebook for Massachusetts Workplace Education Initiative. Boston: Massachusetts Executive Office of Economic Affairs, 1987.

"HR's New Role: Creating Value." *HR Focus* (January 2000): 1.

Hall, Richard H. "Professionalization and Bureaucratization." *American Sociological Review* 33 (1968): 92-104.

Harrison, Bennett and Marcus Weiss. *Workforce Development Networks.* Thousand Oaks: Sage Publications, 1998.

Heckscher, Charles. *White-Collar Blues.* New York: Basic Books, 1995.

Himmelstein, Jerome L. *Looking Good and Doing Good: Corporate Philanthropy and Corporate Power.* Bloomington, IN: Indiana University Press, 1997.

Hofstede, Gert. *Culture's Consequences: International Differences in Work-Related Values.* Beverly Hills: Sage, 1980.

Hollenbeck, Kevin. *Classrooms in the Workplace.* Kalamazoo, MI: W.E. Upjohn Insititute for Employment Research, 1993.

Homans, George C. "Social Behavior as Exchange." *The American Journal of Sociology* (1958): 597-606.

Howard, Robert. *Brave New Workplace.* New York: Penguin Books, 1985.

Hughes, Everett C. "Work and the Self." In *On Work, Race, and the Sociological Imagination*, edited by Lewis Coser. Chicago: University of Chicago Press, 1994.

Indergaard, Michael. "Retrainers as Labor Market Brokers: Constructing Networks and Narratives in the Detroit Area." *Social Problems* 46 (February 1999): 67-84.

"Industry Report." *Training* (October 1990–1999).

Jackall, Robert. *Moral Mazes: The World of Corporate Managers.* New York: Oxford University Press, 1988.

Jackson, Philip W. "The Student's World." *The Elementary School Journal* (April 1966): 345-357.

Jackson, Philip W. *Life in Classrooms.* New York: Holt, Rinehart, and Winston, 1968.

Jackson, Philip W. *The Moral Life of Schools.* San Francisco, CA: Jossey-Bass, 1993.

Johnston, David C. "Gap Between Rich and Poor Found Substantially Wider." *New York Times* (September 5, 1999)14.

Johnston, William B. and Arnold E. Packer. *Workforce 2000: Work and Workers for the Twenty-first Century.* Indianapolis, IN: Hudson Institute, 1987.

Judy, R., Carol D'Amico, and Jared Bernstein. *Workforce 2020: Work and Workers in the 21st Century.* Indianapolis, IN: Hudson Institute, 1997.

Kaestle, Carl E. et al. *Literacy in the United States: Readers and Reading since 1880.* New Haven: Yale University Press, 1991.

Kalleberg, Arne L., David Knoke, Peter Marsden, and Joe L. Spaeth, eds. *Organizations in America: Analyzing Their Structures and Human Resource Practices.* Thousand Oaks: Sage, 1996.

Kalleberg, Arne L. and Torger Reve. "Contracts and Commitment: Economic and Sociological Perspectives on Employment Relations." *Human Relations* 45, no. 9 (1992): 1103-1132.

Katz, Michael. *Reconstructing American Education.* Cambridge: Harvard University Press, 1987.

Kett, Joseph F. *The Pursuit of Knowledge Under Difficulties.* Stanford, CA: Stanford University Press, 1994.

Kettler, David, Meja Volker, and Nico Steher. *Karl Mannheim.* New York: Tavistock, 1984.

Knoke, David and Arne Kalleberg. "Job Training in U.S. Organizations." *American Sociological Review* 59 (1994): 537-546.

Knoke, David and Arne Kalleberg. "Job Training in U.S. Organizations." In *Organizations in America: Analyzing Their Structures and Human Resource Practices.* Edited by Arne Kalleberg et al., 157-179. Thousand Oaks: Sage, 1996.

Knowles, Malcolm S. *The Modern Practice of Adult Education: From Pedagogy to Andragogy.* Chicago: Association Press, 1980.

Kunda, Gideon. *Engineering Culture: Control and Commitment in a High Tech Corporation.* Philadelphia: Temple University Press, 1992.

Lafer, Gordon. "The Politics of Job Training." *Politics and Society* 22, no. 3 (Summer 1994): 349-388.

Larson, Magali Sarfatti. *The Rise of Professionalism: A Sociological Analysis.* Berkeley: University of California Press, 1977.

Lehman, Nicholas. "Grading the Public Schools." *New York Times Book Review* (November 12, 1995): 14-15.

Lewis, Diane E. "English-Only Policies Pit Workers' Rights Against Employers." *The Boston Globe,* July 2, 2000:H8.

Lincoln, James R. and Arne Kalleberg. *Culture, Control and Commitment: A Study of Work Organization and Work Attitudes in the United States and Japan.* New York: Cambridge University Press, 1990.

Lynton, Ernest Albert. *The Missing Connection Between Business and the Universities.* New York: American Council on Education/Macmillan, 1984.

Marcotte, Dave E. *Learning in the Labor Market: The Changing Importance of Education and Training After "Formal" Schooling Ends* (MDS-1275). Berkeley, CA: National Center for Research in Vocational Education, September 1999.

Merton, Robert K. *On Theoretical Sociology: Five Essays, Old and New.* New York: Free Press, 1967.

Meyer, John W. and Brian Rowan. "Institutionalized Organizations: Formal Structure as Myth and Ceremony." *American Journal of Sociology* 83 (1977): 340-363.

Meyer, John W. and Brian Rowan. "The Structure of Educational Organizations." In *Environments and Organizations,* edited by Marshall W. Meyer, 78-109. San Francisco: Jossey-Bass, 1978.

Miller, William H. "The Future? Not Yet." *Industry Week* (April 17, 1995): 73.

Mirvis, Philip H., ed. *Building the Competitive Workforce.* New York: John Wiley and Sons, 1993.

More Than a Job. New Readers Press: New York, n.d.

Moss, Phillip and Chris Tilly. " 'Soft' Skills and Race: An Investigation of Black Men's Employment Problems." *Work and Occupations* 23 (1996): 252-276.

National Center for Educational Statistics. *National Adult Literacy Survey, Executive Summary.* Princeton, NJ: Educational Testing Service, 1993.

National Institute for Literacy Policy Update. Washington, DC: National Institute for Literacy, November 19, 1999.

National Literacy Act, Public Law 102-73, July 25, 1991

Ness, Immanuel. "Organizing Immigrant Communities: UNITE's Workers Center Strategy." In *Organizing to Win: New Research on Union Strategies,* edited by Kate Bronfenbrenner et al. Ithaca, NY: ILR Press, 1998.

Noer, David M. *Healing the Wounds: Overcoming the Trauma of Layoffs and Revitalizing Downsized Organizations.* San Francisco, CA: Jossey-Bass, 1993.

Oliver, Christine. "Strategic Responses to Institutional Processes." *Academy of Management Review* 16, no. 1 (1991): 145-179.

Osterman, Paul. *Securing Prosperity: The American Labor Market: How It Has Changed and What to Do about It.* Princeton, NJ: Princeton University Press, 1999.

O'Toole, James. *Work, Learning, and the American Future.* San Francisco: Jossey-Bass, 1977.

Parker, R. Owen and Teri E. Brown. "People Practices and Shareholder Value," *Ivey Business Journal* 64, no.3 (January 2000):20.

Perrow, Charles. *Complex Organizations: A Critical Essay.* Third Edition. New York: McGraw Hill, 1986.

Persell, Caroline Hodges. "Schools Under Pressure." In *America at Century's End,* edited by Alan Wolfe, 283-297. Berkeley: University of California, 1991.

Pfeffer, Jeffrey and Gerald R. Salancik. *The External Control of Organizations: A Resource Dependence Perspective.* New York: Harper and Row, 1978.

Portes, Alexander. "The Hidden Abode: Sociology as Analysis of the Unexpected." *American Sociological Review* 65 (February 2000): 1-18.

Powell, Walter W. and Elizabeth S. Clemens, eds. *Private Action and Public Good.* New Haven: Yale University Press, 1998.

Powell, Walter W. and Paul J. DiMaggio, eds. *The New Institutionalism in Organizational Analysis.* Chicago: University of Chicago Press, 1991.

Pryor, Frederic L. and David L. Schaffer. *Who's Not Working and Why: Employment, Cognitive Skills, Wages and the Changing U.S. Labor Market.* New York: Cambridge University Press, 1999.

Purcell-Gates, Victoria, S. Degener, and E. Jacobson. *Report #2: Adult Literacy Program Practice: A Typology Across Dimensions of Life-Contextualized/Decontextualized and Dialogic/Monologic.* Cambridge, MA: National Center for the Study of Adult Learning and Literacy, July 1998.

Putnam, Robert D. *Bowling Alone.* New York: Simon & Schuster, 2000.

Raelin, Joseph A. *Work-Based Learning: The New Frontier of Management Development.* Englewood Cliffs, NJ: Prentice Hall, 2000.

Reese, Shelley. "Illiteracy at Work." *American Demographics* 18 (1996): 14-15.

Reich, Robert. *The Work of Nations.* New York: A. A. Knopf, 1991.

Resnik, Henry. "Roots of Literacy." In *Literacy: An Overview by Fourteen Experts,* edited by Stephen R. Graubard. New York: Hill and Wang, 1991.

Rousseau, Denise M. *Psychological Contracts in Organizations.* Thousand Oaks: Sage, 1995.

Rubinson, Richard and Irene Browne. "Education and the Economy." In *The Handbook of Economic Sociology,* edited by Neil J. Smelser and Richard Swedberg. Princeton, NJ: Princeton University Press,1994.

Rumberger, Russell W. *Overeducation in the U.S. Labor Market.* New York: Praeger, 1981.

Ryan, William. *Blaming the Victim.* New York: Vintage, 1976.

Sabel, Charles. "Bootstrapping Reform." *Politics and Society* 23 (1995): 5-48.

Scott, W. Richard and John M. Meyer. "The Rise of Training Programs in Firms and Agencies: An Institutional Perspective." *Research in Organizational Behavior* 13: 297-326. Greenwich, CT: JAI Press, 1991.

Secretary's Commission on Achieving Necessary Skills. *What Work Requires of Schools: A SCANS Report for America 2000.* Washington, DC: U.S. Department of Labor, 1991.

Senge, Peter. *The Fifth Discipline: The Art and Practice of the Learning Organization.* New York: Doubleday, 1990.

Shannon, Patrick, ed. *Becoming Political: Readings and Writings in the Politics of Literacy Education.* Portsmouth, NH: Heinemann, 1992.

Slaughter, Sheila A. and Larry Leslie. *Academic Capitalism: Politics, Policies, and the Entrepreneurial University.* Baltimore: Johns Hopkins University Press, 1999.

Smith, Vicki B. *Managing in the Corporate Interest: Control and Resistance in an American Bank.* Berkeley: University of California Press, 1990.

Smith, Vicki B. "New Forms of Work Organization." *Annual Review of Sociology* 23 (1997): 315-339.

Sperazi, Laura, Paul Jurmo, and David Rosen. "Participatory Approaches to Evaluating Outcomes and Designing Curriculum in Workplace Education Programs." Newton, MA: Evaluation Research Inc., 1991.

Squires, Geoffrey. "Introduction." In *Culture and Processes of Adult Learning: A Reader,* edited by Mary Thorpe, Richard Edwards, and Ann Hanson. New York: Routledge, 1992.

Stasz, Cathleen and Dominic J. Brewer. *Academic Skills at Work, Two Perspectives* (MDS-1193). Berkeley: National Center for Research in Vocational Education, 1999.

Stein, Sondra. *Equipped for the Future: A Reform Agenda for Adult Literacy and Lifelong Learning.* Washington, DC: National Institute for Literacy, 1997.

Stein, Sondra. "Workplace Literacy and the Transformation of the American Workplace: A Model for Effective Practice." Unpublished paper, 1989.

Sticht, Thomas G. "Evaluating National Workplace Literacy Programs." Washington DC: U.S. Department of Education, 1991.

Sticht, Thomas G. *Literacy at Work.* New York: Simon and Schuster Education Group, 1991.

Suchman, Mark C. "Managing Legitimacy: Strategic and Institutional Approaches." *Academy of Management Review* 20 (1995): 571-610.

Sum, Andrew. *Literacy in the Labor Force: Results from the National Adult Literacy Survey* (NCES 1999-470). Washington, DC: U.S. Department of Education, National Center for Education Statistics, 1999.

Teixeira, Roy A. and Lawrence Mishel. "Skills Shortage or Management Shortage?" In *The New Modern Times,* edited by David B. Bills, 193-205. Albany: State University of New York Press, 1995.

Thomas, W. I. *On Social Organization and Social Personality.* Chicago: Chicago University Press, 1966.

Tilly, Chris and Charles Tilly. *Work Under Capitalism.* Boulder, CO: Westview Press, 1998.

Trimbur, John. Cited in Jim Dempsey, "Current Literacy Crisis Is Just the Latest." *Worcester Telegram and Gazette* (February 17, 1992).

Tsang, Mun C., Russell W. Rumberger, and Henry M. Levin. "The Impact of Surplus Schooling on Worker Productivity." *Industrial Relations* 30, no. 2 (1991): 209-228.

U.S. Congress, Office of Technology Assessment. *Worker Training: Competing in the New Economy* OTA-ITE-457. Washington, DC: U.S. Government Printing Office, 1990.

Useem, Michael. "Company Policies on Education and Training." In *Building the Competitive Workforce: Investing in Human Capital for Corporate Success*, edited by Phil Mirvis. New York: John Wiley and Sons, 1993.

Useem, Michael. "Corporate Education and Training." In *The American Corporation Today*, edited by Karl Kaysen. New York: Oxford University Press, 1996.

Vallas, Steven. *Power in the Workplace.* Albany: State University of New York Press, 1993.

Waddock, Sandra and Samuel Graves. "The Corporate Social Performance—Financial Performance Link." *Strategic Management Journal* 18, no. 4 (1997): 303-319.

Walton, Richard E. "From Control to Commitment in the Workplace." *Harvard Business Review* (March-April 1985): 77-84.

Weick, Karl. "Educational Organizations as Loosely Coupled Systems." *Administrative Science Qurterly* 21, no. 1 (1976): 1-19.

"White Paper for 1999 National Literacy Forum," *National Institute for Literacy Policy Update.* Washington, DC: National Institute for Literacy, April 12, 1999.

Wilensky, Harold L. "The Professionalization of Everyone?" *American Journal of Sociology* 2 (1964): 137-158.

Willis, Paul. *Learning to Labor: How Working Class Kids Get Working Class Jobs.* New York: Columbia University Press, 1977.

Zuboff, Shoshana. *In the Age of the Smart Machine: The Future of Work and Power.* New York: Basic Books, 1988.

Index

adult education: debate as to purpose, 14–15; enrollment, 30; as "movement," 33; participatory philosophy, 33–34; public vs. private responsibility for, 19, 37, 108; waiting lists for, 30. *See also* community-based literacy programs; employer-sponsored education; workplace literacy programs

adult educators: benefits from teaching in the workplace, 36, 148; costs associated with teaching in the workplace, 149; importance of teacher quality, 82–83; knowledge base, 35; network, 35–36; as organizational outsiders, 83; professionalization of, 34–37, 44–45 nn.13–14, 16–18, 67–68, 148; resistance and accommodation to business demands, 67–68, 72 n.18; and social responsibility, 36, 44 n.16; working conditions, 34–35

adult learners: benefits from workplace literacy programs, 148;

characteristics, 83–84, 86 n.9 (*see also* ESL; immigrants); desire for "real school," 66, 72 n.17; educational outcomes, 100–103; increased earnings, 102–103; need for basic skills, 29; position at bottom of corporate hierarchy, 106; resistance to education, 138; responsibility for corporate success, 121; social and economic inequalities, 105–106; stigma of illiteracy, 84

andragogy, 34–35

attitudes in the workplace, defined as "soft skills," 5, 17, 24–25 nn.16–18

attitudinal changes, 92–95, 99, 100, 104, 112 n.5; consent, 107–108, 113 n.6; loyalty, 92, 93–95; self-esteem, 95, 100, 108; towards learning, 96–97; towards work, 107

basic skills, 14, 15, 18–19, 149; defined as general education, 4; lacking in

About the Author

MARY-ELLEN BOYLE is an assistant professor at the Clark University Graduate School of Management. An organizational sociologist, she consults with corporations and not-for-profit firms and has taught MBA and undergraduate courses on managing change and conflict, business and society, business ethics, global management, gender and organizations, and the sociology of education. Prior to her academic career, she was employed as a training manager for a large insurance company, and as an educational specialist and grants manager for several state and federal government agencies.